eating and drinking

compass

Christian Explorations of Daily Living

David H. Jensen, Series Editor

eating and drinking

Elizabeth T. Groppe

Fortress Press

Minneapolis

EATING AND DRINKING
Compass series
Christian Explorations of Daily Living

Cover design: Laurie Ingram

Library of Congress Cataloging-in-Publication Data
Groppe, Elizabeth Teresa
  Eating and drinking / Elizabeth T. Groppe.
      p. cm. — (Compass series)
  Includes bibliographical references (p. 119).
  ISBN 978-0-8006-9809-6 (alk. paper)
  1. Food—Religious aspects—Christianity. I. Title.
  BR115.N87G76 2011
  241'.68—dc22

                          2011009346

The paper used in this publication meets the minimum requirements of American National Standard for Information Sciences — Permanence of Paper for Printed Library Materials, ANSI Z329.48-1984.

Manufactured in the U.S.A.
15 14 13 12 11 1 2 3 4 5 6 7 8 9 10

For my parents

John Daniel Groppe and
Rose Marie Nigro Groppe

who gathered our family of seven each evening
around a table spread with the fruits of God's earth
and gave thanks

contents

series foreword

Everyday practices matter for Christian faith. Our ordinary routines—eating, cooking, working, walking, shopping, playing, and parenting—are responses to the life God gives to the world. Christian faith claims that the ordinary materials and practices of human life are graced by God's presence: basic foodstuffs become the Body of Christ in a shared meal, water becomes the promise of new birth as ordinary people gather in Christ's name, and a transformed household becomes a metaphor for God's reign. Bodies, baths, meals, and households matter to Christian faith because God takes these everyday practices and materials as God's own: blessing, redeeming, and transforming them so that they more nearly reflect the hope and grace that come to us in the midst of the everyday. Christian faith does not flee from the everyday but embeds itself in daily, ordinary routines. This book series considers everyday practices as sites for theological reflection. When we pay close attention to everyday practices, we can glimpse classical Christian themes—redemption, creation, and incarnation—in new light. This book series does not attempt to *apply* classical doctrines to particular practices, but to offer narratives of ordinary routines, explore how immersion in them affects Christian life in a global world, and imagine how practice might re-form theology and theology re-form practice.

The series also explores the implications of globalization for daily practices and how these ordinary routines are implicated—for good and for ill—in the often-bewildering effects of an increasingly interconnected world. Everyday practices, after all, are the places where the global becomes local. We encounter globalization not in abstract theory, but in the routine affairs of shopping at the corner grocery for food grown on the other side of the globe, maintaining friendships with persons on other continents, fulfilling job responsibilities in workplaces where decisions ripple outward to seemingly distant neighbors. Daily practices put a human face on the complex phenomenon of globalization and offer one place to begin theological reflection on this phenomenon. Paying close attention to these practices helps unveil the injustice as well as the hope of a global world. Since unreflective and consumptive forms of these daily practices often manifest themselves in American consumer society, this series also offers concrete suggestions for how daily practices might be reconfigured to more nearly reflect the hope and justice given to the world by God's grace. If daily practices implicate our complicity in global injustice, they might also be sites to imagine that world alternatively.

Though each book displays an organization uniquely its own, every title in the series offers three common themes: (1) The books offer thick descriptions of particular practices in North American society. What do parenting, cooking, and dressing look like in American communities in the twenty-first century? (2) The books survey varied Christian understandings of each practice, summoning theological resources for enhanced understanding and critique of typical forms of practice. What have Christians said about eating, dreaming, and traveling throughout their history, and how do their reflections matter today? (3) The books offer a constructive restatement of each practice and explore how ordinary practices might reshape or sharpen beliefs and themes of Christian faith. How does attention to practice affect the way we understand Christian theology, and how does attention to theology affect the way we understand everyday practice? Each book shares the conviction that Christian life is best encountered (and often best understood) in the midst of the ordinary.

Many authors of these volumes are members of the Workgroup in Constructive Theology, an ecumenical group of teachers and scholars who write and teach theology in dialogue with contemporary critiques of Christian traditions. We are diverse in theological and denominational orientation yet share the recognition that Christian theology has often been employed for abusive ends. Theological traditions have silenced women, people of color, the poor, and gay/lesbian/bisexual/transgender (GLBT) persons. Our constructive restatements of Christian practice, therefore, do not simply restate classical Christian traditions, but question them as we learn from them. We listen to the past while we also critique it, just as we hope subsequent generations will also criticize and learn from us. Because so many voices have been silenced throughout the church's history, it is essential that Christian theologians attend to voices beyond the corridors of ecclesial and social power. Outside these corridors, after all, is where Christian faith takes root in ordinary life. Though each of us writes theology somewhat differently—some with explicit schools of theology in mind, such as liberationist or womanist theology— we all share the conviction that theology *matters*, not simply for reflective life, but for the life of the world. Christian theology, at its best, is one expression of life's fullness and flourishing. Our words, in other words, ought to point to a more abundant life of grace in the face of the death-dealing forces at work on an economically stratified and ecologically threatened planet.

We have written each book with a minimum of technical jargon, intending them to be read in a wide variety of settings. The books may be used in seminary and undergraduate courses, including introductions to theology, ethics, and Christian spirituality. Clergy will also find them useful as they seek brief yet substantive books on Christian life that will inform their work of preaching, counseling, and teaching. We also imagine that each text could be used in churches for adult education classes. Many Christians seek guides for how faith is lived but are disenchanted with conservative approaches that shun dialogue with the wider culture of religious diversity. This series offers a progressive, culturally engaged approach to daily practices, globalization, and Christian theology. We think the books are as important in the questions they ask as in the answers they attempt.

David H. Jensen, series editor

preface

Eating and drinking are indispensable to life. Without food, we can live for a week; without drink, we can live for a few days. Yet if we stop eating and drinking altogether we will die. Eating and drinking are not only ordinary practices of human life; they make life possible. Much of our eating and drinking in a consumer society, however, is rather unreflective: we eat and drink what is convenient, what is cheap, what is quick. Many of us eat and drink without considering where our food comes from, whether our eating and drinking habits do more to sustain life or to detract from it, whether our practices of eating and drinking promote the sharing or hoarding of the abundant creation. Elizabeth Groppe's book is a call to pay greater attention to the eating and drinking that sustain our lives. In clear and riveting prose, she uncovers the global interconnections and issues of justice that lie beneath common food and drink in the American diet: bananas, coffee, chocolate, chicken. Her work is also an invitation for us to reconsider the centrality of eating and drinking to Christian faith. As Groppe surveys biblical narratives, she finds eating and drinking in unexpected places. The story of faith, in part, is a story of how food and drink are shared, how God sustains us in the midst of our eating and drinking, how Christ comes to us in a meal. Finally, her work suggests how some of the destructive and unhealthy modes of eating and drinking that characterize a fast-food culture might be renewed and transformed by turning to some ancient practices in the church. Read this book and pay attention as you eat and drink. The table is already set, the feast already prepared.

David H. Jensen

introduction

"You are what you eat," or so the saying goes. Eating, indeed, is an ontological act. We would not exist on this earth were it not for the foods our mothers ate as we grew in their wombs from conception to birth, and we would not have matured into adulthood and continued to survive were it not for the plants and animals that provide us with the elements necessary to live. The practices of eating and drinking, like all of the practices of daily life addressed in this Compass series, shape our characters and our communities; in a real sense, eating and drinking also shape our very being. The food on our kitchen tables becomes our muscles and tissues and bones, and the food of the Eucharist incorporates us into the body of Christ.

We are persons-in-communion who exist by forming our very bodies at table with others through the medium of the fruits of the earth that we share. Practices of eating and drinking can form us as a community that flourishes in the nexus of life-giving relationships. Eating and drinking can also lead to death. The character of our daily practices of eating and drinking is of no small consequence.

Like the other volumes of this series, the book proceeds in three parts. The first chapter is a thick description of the practice of eating and drinking in America in these opening years of the twenty-first century. I describe a day spent eating some of the foods that are typical in our culture and attempt to reflect on their provenance. Because I live in an urban environment disconnected from the land that bears the food that sustains us, and because all of us live in a complex globalized economy, it can be very difficult to determine precisely where our food comes from and under what conditions it was produced. At one time, our land was home to the Cherokee, Navajo, and other peoples who foraged, hunted, fished, and cultivated corn and squash. Later, at the expense of these indigenous peoples, we became a country of immigrant homesteaders with backyard kitchen gardens. Today, most of us are consumers at the end of such complex food chains that it takes the skill of an investigative journalist to determine precisely where our food comes from and how it got from Iowa or Guatemala or Cameroon to our plates. In chapter 1, I draw from the work of Michael Pollan, Fred Pearce, and others in my attempt to educate myself about the way in which my food and drink connect me to people, land, plants, and animals around the globe. These connections, I discover, are often ruptures of communion.

The second chapter presents a Christian theological vision of eating and drinking. The biblical accounts of God's intentions for Eden testify that we were created to live in communion with God, one another, and all of creation. It was an act of eating that violated this communion and led to our exile from paradise. It is also through acts of eating and drinking that communion is restored. The Noahide covenant includes a commandment that requires eating with reverence for life, and the Torah given on Sinai includes specific dietary practices that contribute to the formation of Israel as a holy people. Jesus Christ manifests the messianic reign of God through practices of inclusive table fellowship, meals shared with those who are hungry, parables of feasts held in celebration of the return of the prodigal son, and the gift of bread and wine that is his own body and blood.

Chapter 3 reflects on Christian practices of eating and drinking within our current context. We live in a consumer culture in a world in which hunger and malnutrition haunt the lives of millions of people. Our dominant agricultural systems are ecologically unsustainable, and our planet is rapidly losing the hospitable climate of the Holocene epoch within which the human species developed agriculture and civilization. One of the reasons we have gotten ourselves into such a predicament, observes Kentucky farmer Wendell Berry, is that we have approached the world in mechanical and mercantile terms. A retrieval of the perspectives and practices of Christianity's sacramental ethos can contribute to the construction of a new culture of eating and drinking in this time of crisis in our systems of food and agriculture. Chapter 3 offers reflections on some of the central practices of eating within the Christian tradition: fasting, blessing, sharing bread, extending compassion, turning swords into plowshares, feasting, and giving thanks. I write as a Roman Catholic with a view toward the broader tradition and the conviction that the Jewish and Christian practice of eating as an act of communion offers a compelling alternative to a culture of consumption.

> The Jewish and Christian practice of eating as an act of communion offers a compelling alternative to a culture of consumption.

Because of limitations of length, this book touches only briefly on many topics that deserve much greater attention, and some topics that are central to the everyday practice of eating and drinking are not even mentioned—like the global crisis in fresh drinking water, the impact of our trade policies on subsistence farmers in other nations, and the hotly debated topic of genetically modified foods. I encourage readers to explore further the growing body of literature on the challenges facing multiple dimensions of our food, water, and agricultural systems. Some of this literature is included in the suggestions for further reading, which follow chapter 3. There is also much more that could be said about a Christian theology of eating and drinking, and the bibliographical suggestions offer further sources of reading in this regard as well.

The discussion in chapter 3 of the challenges to our global food supply presumes some familiarity with the literature on climate change. For a variety of reasons, there is a large gap between the scientific discourse on this topic and the understanding of many of us in the general public. If you have not yet had the opportunity to do so, I highly recommend reading one or more basic introductions to climate science, such as these: Elizabeth Kolbert, *Field Notes from a Catastrophe* (New York: Bloomsbury, 2006); Katharine Hayhoe and Andrew Farley, *A Climate for Change: Global Warming Facts for Faith-Based Decisions* (New York: FaithWords, 2009); Richard Miller, ed., *God, Creation, and Climate Change* (Maryknoll, N.Y.: Orbis, 2010); and Lester R. Brown, *World on the Edge: How to Prevent Environmental and Economic Collapse* (New York: Earth Policy Institute, 2011). A readily accessible source of the latest news, analysis, and discussion is the *Yale Environment 360* Web site of the Yale School of Forestry and

Environmental Studies: http://e360.yale.edu/. You can subscribe to the electronic newsletter of the Catholic Climate Covenant at http://catholicclimatecovenant.org/.

I thank series editor David Jensen and Fortress Press editors Michael West and Susan Johnson for the opportunity to participate in this Compass project. Thanks are due as well to Fortress Press project manager Marissa Wold. Work on this book has required me to scrutinize my own personal practices of eating and drinking, and I have learned that they leave much room for improvement. I am grateful to my beloved husband John and son John David for their support and forbearance when the need to write took me away from the family, and I also thank the editors at Fortress for their patience with missed deadlines when pressing family matters took me away from the book.

I am grateful also to my parents, John Daniel and Rose Marie Nigro Groppe. The film *Avalon* traces a European immigrant family's inculturation in America, a process in which festive meals with a large extended family gradually become a hurried dinner for four eaten in front of the television. In *Bowling Alone*, Robert Putnam writes that between 1977 and 1999, the percentage of married Americans who typically eat dinner together as a family declined from 50 to 34 percent.[1] I know now that I cannot take for granted the fact that my parents gathered our family of seven each evening around the dining room table. My mother worked hard to prepare healthful food for a large family on a small budget, and my father began each meal with the reading of a psalm and a prayer of thanksgiving for the blessings of the day and the gift of warm food on the table. This practice has been passed down to children and grandchildren. At a family gathering at my brother's home, an attempt to count the number of place settings to ensure they corresponded to the number of people present was interrupted by my niece Katie, who thought the meal was about to begin without the proper prayer. "The book, Papa!" she exclaimed to my father. "Don't forget the book!" She ran off and returned with my sister-in-law's hefty encyclopedia of veterinary medicine, unaware at age four that all heavy, large volumes are not necessarily the Jerusalem Bible.

As to this little light volume, it is dedicated to my parents with love and gratitude.

1

eating and drinking in america

The alarm is just a small device with a tinny sound, but it feels brutal. The house has a chill, the sun has not yet risen, and somehow I must muster the gumption to separate myself from the warmth of the small child nestled against me and get myself out of bed. Luxuriating on the softness of the cotton pillowcases, I think about the monks and nuns who rise in drafty monasteries for the office of lauds, and about laborers who leave home before dawn for long commutes by foot, bus, train, or car. Forcing myself to get up, I toss the wool coverlet from my body, tuck the sheets and blanket around my sleeping son, and shiver. With a sigh of resignation, I drag myself into the kitchen.

Like any other creature of the mammalian sort, my body must burn calories to generate the energy necessary for its daily activities, and those calories must come from food. Or, to be more precise, those calories must come from the energy released by the nuclear fusion of a star that reaches earth in the form of solar radiation and is then photosynthesized by plants. In the grand biological scheme of things, I am classified strictly as a "consumer"—as distinct from a producer or a decomposer—since I take my nourishment from species that produce life directly from the energy of the sun and then become food for others.

My practice of eating and drinking is shaped not only by the parameters of biology but also by human convention. Human practices of eating and drinking take place within the powerful nexus of nature and culture, the juncture of earth's bounty and the development of the human ability to cultivate and prepare foods. Biologically I am a consumer, and culturally I am a consumer of the North American sort. Today I intend to eat and drink the more or less everyday fare of the more or less average American and to endeavor to learn something about its provenance, often hidden from us across the reaches of our globalized economy. There is, of course, no such thing as an average American. Each one of us is a unique person with a unique identity, unique history, and unique place within the heart of God. But certain forms of food and drink predominate in our culture and shape our relationships to other persons, other creatures, and the earth. One of these forms of drink is coffee.

Coffee

The kettle is whistling on the stove, and I rush from the bathroom with hair dripping wet to quiet the shrill steam. Rummaging in the cupboard, I find a mug with a weave of bright red, green, blue, and yellow colors set against a black background. The mug was a gift from my sister, selected because its design suggests a Central American tapestry. I pour the steamy water into the cup and hold it with both hands, relishing the warmth as twirls of steam rise into the air.

In the spice cupboard, there is a small jar of coffee crystals, and I unscrew the bright red lid and release the fragrant aroma of crushed coffee beans. Hmmmmmmmmm.

I have never been much of a coffee drinker, but I have always loved the smell of the brew made from these dark crystals. After Mass on Sunday in the parish of my childhood, the aroma wafted through the church basement where we gathered for doughnuts and fellowship.

The crushed beans in the plastic jar are chocolate in color. Most granules are dull, but some have the crystalline glint of diamonds. The directions on the label instruct me to pour one heaping spoonful into my mug and to mix with boiling water. I stir, inhaling the earthy aroma that swirls around me and throughout the kitchen.

If the scented steam were a jet stream that could mark the path of the coffee bean's journey to my home, it would lead me ultimately to northeastern Africa. The coffee tree is indigenous to Ethiopia, and its fruit was first eaten as a food sometime between 575 and 850 C.E. According to a popular legend, the stimulating qualities of coffee were discovered by Kaldi the goatherd, who noticed that his flocks broke into a frolic after munching on the cherry-like fruits. After sampling the berries himself, Kaldi incorporated visits to the coffee grove into his daily pastoral routine, a practice that caught the attention of a monk from a nearby monastery. The monk happily discovered that the boiled red berries made a drink that helped his brothers stay awake during long religious services.

I sip this black brew while muddling around, trying to gather the things I will need to get myself and my family out the door to preschool and to work. The Ethiopian monks remind me that I should be praying as I go about my muddling. "O Lord, have mercy on me a sinner." Where is that book I need for class today? Oh, there it is, under that stack of papers on the desk. And where are John David's mittens? Oh, of course, right there—in the old shoe box with the crayon collection. Where else?

Another sip from the watery black liquid, and I can feel the warmth percolate through me. How did this elixir get from Ethiopia to Cincinnati? One of the first major global migrations of coffee occurred through the spread of Islam. Coffee was cultivated in Yemen in 575 C.E., and legend has it that the angel Gabriel appeared to the ailing Muhammad in a dream and told him that the small red fruits of the coffee tree would heal his ills and stimulate prayer. The aromatic berries then spread throughout the Arabian Peninsula. "Coffee," wrote Sheikh Ansari Djezeri Hanball Abd-al-Kadir in a paean in 1587, "is the drink of the friends of God, and of his servants who seek wisdom."[1]

Pilgrims from India and spies from Holland clandestinely carried coffee plants beyond the Arab world. In 1650, the first English coffeehouse opened in the university town of Oxford, and at about the same time, similar establishments opened in Italy. Coffee production became central to the colonial enterprises of the English, French, Dutch, and Portuguese, and forested lands in Africa and the Americas were cleared to make way for coffee plantations. Beans were shipped back to Europe, where coffeehouses frequented by people of all classes became places where one could exchange, according to William Ukers, "choice bits of scandal."[2]

Today coffee still links people of different classes and bears the traces of its colonial history. Consumed religiously in wealthy countries, the red jeweled fruit that bears the coffee bean within its flesh is typically cultivated in impoverished former colonies around the globe. One-fifth of this coffee is consumed in the United States. "In a society that combines buzzing overstimulation with soul-aching meaninglessness," *The Coffee Book* explains, "coffee and its associated rituals are, for many of us, the lubricants that make it possible to go on."[3]

The label on the jar in my kitchen offers no indication as to the origins of my coffee or the journey it has taken to arrive here. A coffee bean can change hands over a hundred times en route from tree to table, and my coffee might have been grown in one of more than two dozen different countries, in a variety of different circumstances. In Guatemala, whose colorful tapestries were the inspiration for the design on my mug, there are coffee growers who own large acreage and mills, small growers who cultivate a few acres and then sell their coffee to mill owners for washing and drying, and seasonal coffee laborers. At harvest time, these laborers work from dawn to dusk, gathering by hand the coffee berries that must be plucked at just the right moment of ripeness. I have never been to Guatemala, but through the digital connections of the Internet, I have seen photographs of Guatemalan laborers. Their feet are bare, and the bright colors of their hand-woven garments reflect the flora and fauna of the highlands. Entire families work together, securing sacks or baskets around their waists and filling them painstakingly with coffee berries. Their pay is a few dollars a day. How do their feet feel at the end of the workday? When they sit down to rest from their labor, what do they eat and drink? Where do they sleep? How is their life experienced by a child? Do they suffer from the effects of chemicals that are often used in coffee cultivation—chemicals such as DDT, malathion, and benzene hexachloride that are banned in the U.S. for suspected carcinogenicity?[4] What, I wonder, is the lubricant that enables them to go on?

Typically, I learn, it takes the harvest from an entire coffee tree to produce just one pound of coffee beans. Nonetheless, in 2002, global coffee production exceeded consumption by more than 500,000 tons. When Vietnam and Brazil dramatically increased their coffee cultivation, the market for Guatemala's number one export fell flat. Beans were selling at seven cents a pound below the cost of production. Subsistence farmers with small acreage could not sustain themselves, and seasonal laborers could not find work. Many made the perilous journey that transforms indigenous people with strong connections to their native soil into landless undocumented immigrants in the United States. Others joined the shantytowns in Mexico City. When journalist Sam Quinones visited a Mexican shantytown, one of many unintentional products of the global economy, he was overwhelmed by the fumes of burning plastic. With very limited electricity and inadequate wood for cooking, people resort to using plastic soda bottles for fuel. The result is a constant acrid, fetid smell—"the smell," writes Quinones, "of total desperation."[5]

My cup is empty, but my kitchen is still redolent with the robust fragrance of fresh coffee.

Breakfast

Even after ten hours of sleep, John David is no more eager than I was to rouse himself from the comfort and warmth of the bed.

"What day is it this day, Mama?" he asks sleepily.

"A preschool day, honey."

"No, Mama!"

He is awake now, and protests both the system of education outside the home and my attempt at mobility. I gather him into my arms, amazed at the strength in the small arms that are anchored resistantly onto the pillows. I carry him to the kitchen table and let him lean quietly against me as he slouches sleepily on the chair.

The ensuing part of my experiment in eating the everyday fare of the everyday American is the source of no small misgivings, as it entails exposing my son to a form of cuisine from which I have attempted to protect him. John David, for his part, is intrigued by the colorful box on the table.

"I want that, Mama!" he points.

A smiling character meets his gaze over the lip of the cereal bowl. He cannot read the promises on the box about calcium, vitamin D, and whole grains, but the pictures definitely have his rapt attention.

I tear open the top of the cardboard box, pull apart the cellophane wrapper, and peer in at the dry cereal. It has no smell, and its color is pale in comparison to the bright reds, blues, and greens on the outside of the package. As I pour, the cereal clinks against the sides of the bowl, which quickly fills with feather-light pieces of ground grain speckled in brown and frosted in a white coating. The tan shapes have myriad forms: bells, trees, Xs, and flowers. John David, however, has eyes only for the pastel pieces of dry marshmallow that give color to the array. "Yook [Look], Mama!" he points at the pink and purple and light green shapes. I nod and pour creamy white milk into the bowl, and a rising tide lifts the marshmallow boats.

John David dives in with his spoon. Scooping up some pale oat shapes and blue moons swimming against a background of milk, he crunches and chews. Dipping his silver wand back into the bowl, he scoops up another spoonful of floating forms. As he opens his mouth to take a bite, I am stunned to see that his entire tongue is now the same pastel blue as the marshmallow moons. His little white teeth are also coated in blue—after just one bite. I really don't want him to continue eating this. Hasn't my experiment in children's breakfast cereal gone far enough? But back goes his spoon into the bowl, chasing a pink heart, and then a green leaf.

And then, to my astonishment, he pushes his cereal bowl toward me. He helps himself to my bowl of oatmeal and says, "Yet's [Let's] trade." I truly can't believe this. But here I am facing a bowl of miniature bells and trees. The marshmallows are bleeding their colors into the milk, and the dull tan oat shapes are floating in a grayish-green pool. I fish for a spoonful of cereal. The oat bells and Xs are so soggy they dissolve in my mouth, but the marshmallow moons still have some chewable substance. The overwhelming taste is that of a sugary blue sweetness.

According to a 2008 analysis of *Consumer Reports*, eleven popular breakfast cereals contain at least 40 percent sugar by weight.[6] In other words, if the cereal box were a scale with the ability to automatically sort and weigh its own contents, and if you drew a dark black line just shy of midway up the box, everything up to this line would be sugar. The particular kind of cereal I have just eaten was not included in this consumer study. Its number one ingredient by weight, according to the panel on the side of the box, is whole grain oats. But the number two ingredient is marshmallows (made of sugar, corn syrup, and dextrose—three kinds of sugar). And the number three ingredient is sugar, and the number five ingredient is corn syrup.

I am struck not only by the fact that sugar appears in one form or another five times on the list of ingredients, but that three of the five forms of sugar mentioned in this list are corn derivatives. Those of us who gather our food from the shelves of North American supermarkets, explains Michael Pollan in *The Omnivore's Dilemma*, an account of his own journey to discover the origin of our meals, are in a very real sense "corn walking." Many of the products on the shelves of our groceries derive from corn, even though it may take an investigative journalist to trace complex industrial food chains back to the seeds of a tall tropical grass.

Pollan recounts the history of agricultural practices and federal policies that have converted the quilted patterns of oats, hay, corn, legumes, vegetables, and orchards that once marked America's heartland into monoculture seas of corn and soybeans. Pastures where cows and horses once grazed have nearly disappeared, making way for the hybrid corn and soy that are now planted fencerow to fencerow. The conversion of so much acreage to corn, coupled with the use of hybrid seeds and the application of fertilizers derived from fossil fuels, has resulted in an average national harvest of ten billion bushels of corn per year. Divided equally among all Americans, this is approximately one ton of corn per person. This does not include the corn on the cob we relish in July; sweet corn or white corn is a very small percentage of the annual production. The corn that is grown by the billions of bushels is No. 2 yellow corn, and it is inedible by human beings.

At least, that is, in pure form. About one-fifth of the golden mountain of corn Pollan beheld at the Iowa Farmers' Cooperative was taken to wet milling plants, which he describes as a humanly constructed industrial-strength digestive tract—a maze of sealed vats, pipes, fermentation tanks, valves, and spigots. The first step in the milling procedure is to soak the corn for thirty-six hours in a bath of water tinted with sulfur dioxide. This facilitates the separation of the yellow skin (a rich source of vitamins), the germ (the source of corn oil), and the endosperm (the largest part of the kernel and the store of complex carbohydrates). The endosperm is crushed into a white mush called mill starch. Grinders, filters, centrifuges, and enzymes then convert this mush into an array of different fractions, including gluten, cornstarch, glucose, fructose, citric and lactic acid, maltodextrin, sorbitol, mannitol, xanthan gum, dextrin, and cyclodextrin. Several of these fractions appear on the list of ingredients of the cereal I have just served to my son.

What about Blue No. 1, the food dye that changed the color of John David's tongue? Color, I learn, is an important dimension of the appeal of food, the sight of which fires neurons in the hypothalamus. But blue food rarely occurs in nature—there are no leafy blue greens, no edible blue roots, and no blue fowl or fish that we eat. Even anthocyanins, the compounds that make blueberries "blue," are actually red. According to *Color Matters*, when our ancestors foraged for their food in the open air, blue, purple, and black were warning signs of potentially lethal substances.

This warning signal is apparently transmitted from generation to generation culturally rather than genetically, because my four-year-old shows no innate aversion to blue marshmallow moons. But how did these moons turn such a hue, if blue food color does not occur naturally? According to the Electronic Code of Federal Regulations:

> [The] color additive FD&C Blue No. 1 is principally the disodium salt of ethyl[4-[p -[ethyl(m -sulfobenzyl) amino]-α-(o -sulfophenyl)benzylidene]-2,5-cyclohex-

adien-1-ylidene](*m*-sulfobenzyl)ammonium hydroxide inner salt with smaller amounts of the isomeric disodium salts of ethyl[4-[*p* -[ethyl(*p* -sulfobenzyl)amino]-α-(*o* -sulfophenyl)benzylidene]-2,5-cyclohexadien-1-ylidene](*p* -sulfobenzyl)ammonium hydroxide inner salt and ethyl[4-[*p* -[ethyl(*o* -sulfobenzyl)amino]-α-(*o* -sulfophenyl)benzylidene]-2,5-cyclohexadien-1-ylidene](*o* -sulfobenzyl)ammonium hydroxide inner salt. Additionally, FD&C Blue No. 1 is manufactured by the acid catalyzed condensation of one mole of sodium 2-formylbenzenesulfonate with two moles from a mixture consisting principally of 3-[(ethylphenylamino)methyl] benzenesulfonic acid, and smaller amounts of 4-[(ethylphenylamino) methyl] benzenesulfonic acid and 2-[(ethylphenylamino)methyl] benzenesulfonic acid to form the leuco base. The leuco base is then oxidized with lead dioxide and acid, or with dichromate and acid, or with manganese dioxide and acid to form the dye. The intermediate sodium 2-formylbenzenesulfonate is prepared from 2-chlorobenzaldehyde and sodium sulfite.

I am stunned to read in *Chemical and Engineering News* that what all of this—or at least a part of this—means is that Blue No. 1, also known as brilliant blue, is a triphenylmethane derived from petroleum.

Midmorning Energy Break

This morning, I did finish the cereal that my son pushed aside. I am not long in the office, however, before I feel a tightening in my stomach. Without leaving the chair of my desk, I swivel around, reach into my canvas tote bag, and extract a pair of bananas. Their thick rubbery skin feels cool to my hands. They still have the same bright yellow that shone like the sun when they were perched on the top of the fruit basket in the kitchen this morning, but they were bruised in the jaunt to work and are now spotted with brownish gray patches. The two bananas are joined at the top by a remnant of the woody band that once held together an entire bunch, and when I pull the pair apart, a clear fluid flows from the place where the band is broken. With a sharp angular tug, I crack the stem of one of the bananas, revealing the nib of the creamy fruit. I pull the stem down like a zipper, and it carries along one strand of the banana peel, providing an opening for me to peel the other two strands of skin, which come readily apart. The outer layer of the banana unfurls so easily that it almost invites me to eat the soft cylindrical fruit within.

The banana tastes like—well, banana! It is smooth of texture and delicately sweet with a pale but distinct flavor. Soft, it offers no resistance and almost dissolves in my mouth. Where each bite is taken, I can see a star shape radiating out from the center of the fruit, each line of the star marking one of its five sectors. One bite quickly follows another, and soon a limp peel lies clumped on my desk. The creamy inner side of the peel is quickly turning the color of the bruised exterior, which is rapidly turning an even deeper leathery brown.

The banana gives every appearance of being a wholesome and healthy snack. It is rich in potassium and complex carbohydrates. It has not been dyed blue with a petroleum derivative. It does not come from fractions of industrially refined corn. It is not wrapped in plastic or commercial packaging of any kind. Botanist Carl Linnaeus, the father of taxonomy and a religious man, named the green banana *Musa paradisiaca*—"the banana of paradise." In India, Hindus know the fruit as *kalpathan*, which means "virtuous plant."

In the summer, a small banana tree grows in the perennial garden that encircles Bellarmine Chapel on the campus of Xavier University in Cincinnati, Ohio, where I work. The tree was a gift of an alumnus of the university. When the weather is warm, the tree's wide green leaves broaden like fans. In late fall, a groundskeeper transplants the tree into a large pot and then takes it indoors for the winter. *Musa paradisiaca* is a strictly tropical creature. In its proper place, some species can reach a height of thirty feet. Here, transplanted back and forth among the midwestern coneflowers in the chapel garden, it tops off at about eight.

Archeological evidence indicates that bananas were cultivated since 5000 B.C.E. in the highlands of Papua New Guinea in Southeast Asia. From the jungles of the regions now known as Thailand, Malaysia, and Myanmar, the plants somehow migrated to India, where the first extant written records of human propagation of the plant date to 500 B.C.E. Middle Eastern armies and traders carried banana plants to Africa, and colonial Portuguese soldiers transported bananas from Guinea to the Canary Islands. Father Tomás de Berlanga, a Spanish Dominican missionary, carried the banana to the Caribbean. Today, it is one of the most important sources of food for the earth's population of some 6.9 billion people; the only crops grown in larger quantities are wheat, rice, and corn. In the countries that border Africa's Lake Victoria, the Swahili word for food is also the word for banana. Millions of people depend on bananas to keep them alive.

For me, a banana is a nutritious snack I can enjoy while working at the computer. How did this tropical fruit (or this berry of a large herb, to be scientifically precise) get to Cincinnati? Where did it come from, and how did it travel so far without a blemish? The two bananas I brought to work were bruised in just the short jaunt from home to office.

The global journey of the banana is charted by Dan Koeppel in *Banana: The Fate of the Fruit That Changed the World*. The first commercial shipment of bananas to reach the shores of the United States, he explains, docked at Jersey City in 1870, an unplanned consequence of a leaky sailboat. Lorenzo Dow Baker, a bearded New England seafarer, stopped in Jamaica for repairs on his northward return from a trip to take gold miners to Venezuela. Large green bunches of bananas caught his eye, and he decided to take a chance that wind and weather would cooperate with his desire to purchase the fruit for resale in the States. He arrived in New Jersey in eleven days with cargo still fresh enough to sell for $2 a bunch and a profit equivalent to $6,400 in twenty-first-century dollars.

So began the banana trade that would shape the lives of so many persons in the nations of Central America, South America, and the Caribbean. Baker bought land in Jamaica and within a year was the largest banana exporter in the region. He was joined by Andrew Preston, who developed a means of cold transport for banana cargo. Meanwhile, Joseph Vaccaro established a rival enterprise. The two firms, which incorporated as Boston Fruit and Standard Fruit respectively, expanded their land holdings and transport systems, and bananas became a staple on the shelves of North American produce vendors.

North Americans took readily to the sweet yellow fruit. The country was rapidly urbanizing, and the thick-skinned banana was a good convenience food that nestled easily into the brown bags and lunch pails of the industrial workforce. Bananas were not only convenient, but also cheap. In 1913, 25 cents could purchase two apples or a full dozen bananas. Still today, apples grown in an orchard in Rittman, Ohio, are $1.39 per pound at my grocery, while bananas from Ecuador scan at a mere 49 cents a pound. Americans today eat more bananas per year than apples and oranges combined.

Did Bostonians or Chicagoans ever stop to wonder how a highly perishable tropical fruit grown thousands of miles away was available to them at a cost far below that of the apples grown on farms that once surrounded these cities? Do I ever stop to wonder why bananas from Ecuador or Honduras are one-third the cost per pound of apples from North Central Ohio? I really had not paused to ponder this before reading Koeppel's book. Surely, others have. But most North Americans, Koeppel believes, have enjoyed motion pictures of Charlie Chaplain slipping on the banana peels that came to litter our city streets without realizing that the ubiquity of cheap bananas in the north required the development of the first large-scale produce industry— an industry that has controlled not only transportation and delivery but also foreign lands and peoples. The rapidly expanding banana companies leveled acre after acre of virgin rain forest in a manner that Koeppel describes as "marauding." The corporations did build schools and hospitals for the workers on the banana plantations, but they also relied on the U.S. military to ensure supportive local governments and quell movements for justice. In 1918 alone, U.S. forces suppressed strikes in Panama, Colombia, and Guatemala. Count Vay de Vaya, who traveled the region as a representative of Pope Benedict XV, described the banana as "a weapon of conquest."[7]

The bananas on our grocery shelves are not only notably inexpensive but also remarkably uniform. Whether the bananas in my tote bag come from a national chain or a neighborhood grocer, and whether they are purchased in June or December, they have that same familiar banana-y shape, texture, color, and taste. Every banana I have ever eaten from my infancy until today's midmorning snack is, indeed, genetically identical. The efficient transport of bananas from south to north requires a uniform fruit that ripens on a consistent timetable, and Boston Fruit, Standard Fruit, and their multiple successor companies developed the first grand-scale global monoculture. The banana was very obliging to this enterprise, for it reproduces asexually by sending out daughter shoots from corms at its base, and the DNA of each shoot is identical to that of the parent plant.

Although there are a thousand types of bananas in the world, the sole variety that was cultivated and imported in fleets of large refrigerated ships from 1870 into the 1960s was the Gros Michel. Those who remember this fruit describe it as a banana that was larger, thicker, and creamier than the bananas we know today, with a more intense and fruity taste. Curious to try it? You will not find the Gros Michel on any fruit stand in North or South America. It was decimated in plantation after plantation, nation by nation from the Caribbean to Asia, by a soil-borne fungus named Panama disease after the place where the blight originated.

Every plant on earth is susceptible to numerous diseases. Monocultures, however, are especially vulnerable to devastation, because there is no gene pool of alternative varieties that might be able to withstand a particular pathogen. The monoculture of the Gros Michel spanned the tropics, and Panama disease marched across an entire hemisphere. Initially, the banana industry responded by pulling up stakes in infected plantations and replanting new stock in uninfected land. But eventually the blight outpaced them.

The fruit companies then resorted to the Cavenish, the variety of banana found today in my tote bag and on supermarket shelves from San Diego to Boston. It is smaller and less flavorful than the Gros Michel, but is equally transportable and, most importantly, immune to Panama disease. Or so it was believed. As it turns out, the Cavenish was resistant only to the particular strain of Panama disease that blackened the leaves of the Gros Michel trees. It is vulnerable to another strain of the blight, which is today spreading through Pakistan, the Philippines, and Indonesia. The disease is also on the rise in Africa, where many parents depend on bananas to keep themselves and their children alive. For me, the banana is simply a convenient midmorning snack.

Lunch

I hopscotch across asphalt stained with patches of leaked oil and car coolant, trying to avoid stepping on the slick patches. Wafts of the familiar smell of fried food float through the parking lot and draw me through the swinging glass doors. On any given day, 25 percent of the people in the United States eat in a restaurant such as this. Under bright fluorescent lighting, I stand in line and follow the flow across a tile floor and around the cordons that efficiently compress a large group of people into a small space. No one before me or behind me says a word as we inch along, our bodies moving as one fragmented snake.

I glance above the counter at colorful placards that present the array of choices from which I must select my meal. There appears to be a dizzying selection, but on closer examination, it is evident that everything is a variation on a few themes: beef, chicken, fried potatoes, soda, and shakes, each priced at some figure ending with 9. As I advance in the line, I pass a wall display holding free copies of volume 19, issue 10 of "Toyland," a pamphlet for children. The colorful cover features a family of plastic toys, one of which may be served with lunch. The last page promises, "ONE TOY IN EVERY KIDS MEAL. WHILE SUPPLIES LAST."

Every member of the restaurant staff working briskly behind the counter is wearing the mandatory black polyester shirt, slacks, and cap. Some scurry to fill orders at the drive-up window, trying to keep pace with the cars and SUVs. Others drop baskets of frozen potatoes into vats of 340-degree oil. All of the workers are African American, and I wonder how the particular form of food preparation in which they are now engaged compares with that practiced by their African ancestors—who are also ultimately the ancestors of all humanity, if you trace our lineage far enough back.

"Can I help you?" asks the attendant at the counter. I am assured by signs on the menu board that I can order whatever I want and have it prepared in any manner I desire. But is what I really desire even here? "A small hamburger," I say, "a side salad, fries, and a small shake."

"That's a value meal," the attendant at the next computer register tells my clerk. "Ring it up as a value meal."

My clerk stands by his order entry.

"Look up at the chart," the other clerk points. "She ordered a value meal."

"No," I explain. "I ordered a small hamburger, a side salad, fries, and a small shake. He rang it up just the way I asked."

"I know," said the other clerk, "but when you order a sandwich, a drink, and fries, we are trained to tell you that this is a value meal."

My value meal costs $4.59.

"For here or to go?"

"For here," I respond, and I wait with my receipt in hand for the various components of my lunch to be assembled with an efficiency that would do Frederick Taylor proud. A hamburger, like a Ford motor car, has interchangeable parts.

My meal is served on a bright blue tray with the logo of the restaurant emblazoned on the center. It slides to and fro as I walk carefully past the condiment counter and its fountain of sweet ketchup. I settle into a booth cushioned with bars cut from vinyl fabric in bright primary colors. There are also splashes of blue, red, and yellow on the paintings that hang on the gray walls. From my seat, I have a perfect view of cars and SUVs inching through the drive-through line.

The french fries are irresistible, and before I have even settled into my seat, I have popped one into my mouth. "Instant Fry Satisfaction," says the bright red packet in which the fries are nestled, although as I read further, I realize that this promise is not for me but for the drivers of the vehicles with engines idling outside. "Don't delay what you want right away. Slap this puppy into your car cup holder and go to town on some hot and crispy fries."

I dash another french fry into my mouth, and another and another. On the outside, the fries are golden, the color of royalty; inside, they are pure fluffy white. The crisp gold layer is so hot it burns my tongue, so I press through quickly to the cooler soft interior and swallow. I eat another, and another, and another, moving the piping hot fries from tray to mouth, sometimes in clusters of two or three at a time. The golden potato ribbons cool rapidly from their high point of 340 degrees, and their taste and appeal diminish with their falling temperature. By the time I reach the little fragments at the bottom of the red carton, they are lukewarm and taste more like oil than the golden food of royalty.

What's next? My hamburger is veiled in a thin paper wrapper that holds its component parts together. I am eating in solitude, and this packaging clearly marks this meal as mine and mine alone. It is as if someone I do not know has given me a gift wrapped in colored tissue just for me. The wrapper is also a sort of compensation for my lack of company. When I flip the burger over to untuck the ends of the tissue paper, it speaks to me. "Have you ever stopped to think," the wrapper asks, "what makes this burger so unique and delicious? Don't. You should be eating."

OK, if you insist. I hold the sandwich with two hands, bite down, and taste the tart, crisp pickle, the cream of mayonnaise, and the gristle of beef. I am not very skilled at the art of burger eating, and the innards are already starting to leak out the sides. I flip the sandwich open and lay the circles of the top and bottom of the thin white bun adjacent to each other like an open pocket watch. The top of the bun is smothered with a blotchy blur of white, green, and red—mayonnaise, lettuce, and ketchup—and resembles the modern artworks that hang on the surrounding walls. White strands of onion hang over the edges like flailing arms, and the burger itself is brownish gray with a charred black coating. Where I have taken a bite, I can see little circular pieces of gristle. A chunky piece of the core of a head of iceberg lettuce impedes my attempt at a smooth reconstitution of the burger, so I pick this out.

"The unofficial record for unwrapping a burger," the package says, "is .76 seconds. Can you beat that?"

I wonder what the record is for taking a burger apart and putting it back together. I take a nibble, and it leaves a taste of char in my mouth.

As I turn to my salad, I try to make out the words that accompany the rhythms of the drums and electric guitars in the music being piped into the dining area. A chorus of "No, no, no, no, no, no, no, no, no, no" is all I can decipher. No, no, no, no—no more french fries—alas, alas, they are all gone. But the salad looks a promising shade of green. It comes in a circular container with a black plastic bottom and a clear plastic lid that bears the restaurant's logo. A sticker on top says, "FROZEN READY FRI USE THROUGH SAT." Frozen? I have never had a frozen salad before. I lift the lid and find two baby carrots, a slice of tomato, and a generous serving of iceberg lettuce. The salad is accompanied by a packet of honey mustard dressing that, judging by a simple hand measurement, weighs more than the ingredients of the salad and its plastic container combined. Some pieces of lettuce are crystallized, as if they have indeed been frozen and thawed, but they are still crisp, and the bright orange carrots are crunchy and sweet. The chocolate shake that I suck through a straw is thick, sweet, and creamy.

Across the aisle, a family is eating a meal. The tables and benches in the restaurant are so small, and the adults so large, that the group is spread over four tables. At one booth, a father and small girl in pink tights sit across from each other, sipping soda from straws. They are separated by a metal bar from the mother and the son, who appears to be eight or nine years old. At the booths on either side, there are two very large bearded men, in proportion to whom each table seems almost like dollhouse furniture. They are silent partners in the family conversation.

"That's why she always acts like that," the mother shoots across the metal bar to the father. "You let her do whatever she wants."

"Shut up," he replies.

"And then he tells me to shut up."

I am finished with my value meal and carry the tray to the garbage bin. I press the swinging door of its gaping mouth inward and dump the paper cup, plastic salad container, salad lid, french fry carton, and burger wrapping into the darkness of the unseen receptacle below.

I gather my things and find myself holding the door for the family of six, who have also finished their meal. "Did you know," I overhear the son tell the father as they exit the restaurant, "that Jewish people don't eat cheeseburgers?"

"No," says the father as he zips up his coat, "where did you hear that?"

They disappear into the parking lot.

Upon my return to the office, I stop at the water fountain in the hallway to take a long draught. The sticky sweetness of the chocolate shake has left me very thirsty. I drink, and drink again, and still feel an uncomfortable itch in my throat.

Back at my desk, I notice that the pamphlet for children, which I have taken with me from the restaurant, includes a phone number for consumer relations. I dial the number, and the phone rings on the other end.

"For English," an electronic voice says, "press one. For Spanish, press two. For French, press three; for . . ."

I press one, and it isn't long before I do hear a human voice, although she cannot answer my question about the origins of the beef that was in the hamburger I was served. I have read that the richly biodiverse Amazon region has been deforested to provide land to pasture cattle and grow feedcrops, and that here in the United States, cattle raised for beef often live in Concentrated Animal Feeding Operations (CAFOs) in conditions that are detrimental to both the cattle and the surrounding environment.[8] The consumer relations staff person explains that the source of beef is a matter of local distribution and that I should contact the office of the particular restaurant where I dined. She gives me the number of the franchise, which I call.

"I'm sorry," the local office tells me, "but for that information, you need to call the national consumer relations office."

So I call them back. "Thank you for calling the consumer relations department," a recording says again. "All of our agents are currently helping other customers. Your call will be answered in the order that it was received."

"What?" a woman named Sarah says when I finally reach a human voice and repeat my question about the origins of the beef in the hamburger.

"Where did the meat come from?" I rephrase the question. "What part of the country? Or what other continent? How were the cattle raised? How were they treated?"

"Um . . . ," says Sarah after a pause. "It's Angus beef. I don't know who our suppliers are. I don't have that handy."

Afternoon Snack

I should, I know, stay focused on the stack of midterm exams here on my desk, but my mind is numb after reading fifteen versions of Thomas Aquinas's account of the goodness of creation. Moreover, I hear the commanding voice of *Theobroma cacao*, the food (*broma*) of the gods (*theos*). It speaks directly to my gnawing ache. I can almost but not quite taste the dark sweetness in my mouth. "God," said Aquinas, "brought things into being in order that the divine goodness might be communicated to creatures through . . . chocolate . . ."

Something must be done before I start writing this on the exams. I push through piles of paper clips in my desk drawer, looking for some spare change, silver pieces that can serve my mission.

The nearest vending machine is in the library, just a few short paces across the academic mall. It is in the basement in a lounge area at the bottom of a stairwell, and at the moment, no one is there but me. The machine is a large box with black sides and a glass front, through which beckon an array of colorful, glossy little packages. Inside the machine, electric lights burn vigilantly, illuminating from within the tabernacle of candy. Little green electronic dots of light dance in a line by the slot to the right, signaling the place where I am to insert my silver coins. Each one rolls into the machine, disappears from view, and clinks.

Hmmmmmmmmmmmm. Chocolate with nuts, or chocolate with caramel, or chocolate-covered wafers, or straight, pure chocolate. I press a button, a spiral wire inches forward, and a bag of chocolate-covered nuts drops down into a receptacle. I reach through a flap and extract a glossy pouch, tuck it snugly into the pocket of my jacket, and return to my desk.

Before I am even fully seated in my swivel chair, I rip the top from the packet and pop a piece of candy into my mouth. Crunch! I can taste simultaneously the smooth sweetness of the chocolate and the heartiness of the nut. I press another round nugget through the hole I have made in the pouch. And another. And another. And another. And another. And another. I should not eat these all at once, I think, as I fish around the bottom of the pouch and find another piece that I nudge up through the opening. And then I fish again. And again. "Really," I tell myself, "you should show some restraint."

I press harder against the flattened pouch. Isn't there one more piece of chocolate tucked away in there somewhere? I can find nothing.

The dark cocoa beans from which my chocolate is made were collected in coffers by the Aztecs in sixteenth-century Central America. The emperor Montezuma made a drink from these beans considered to be the food of the gods. The Spanish conquistador Hernán Cortés sipped of Montezuma's cup, but it was the British explorer Sir Hans Sloane who tasted a similar drink in Jamaica and brought the cocoa bean to Europe in the late seventeenth century. Sir Hans Sloane's Milk Chocolate seduced the British palate, and as the British Empire spread across the globe, so did cocoa plantations.

Today, more than 40 percent of the world's cocoa is grown in the West African state of Ivory Coast. The most profitable manner of cultivation consists of large monoculture plantations, row after row of tall shrubs with emerald leaves and amber pods that hold the pearl of great price. These monocultures of cocoa give high yields, but at the expense of damaged soils, the loss of the biodiversity of jungle ecosystems, and susceptibility to disease.

In 2000, Ivory Coast made the news when an investigation by the BBC found that destitute parents of children in countries like Mali, Burkina Faso, and Togo were selling their children to traffickers with the assumption that they would find work in this West African state. Upon arrival, hundreds of thousands of youth were sold into the servitude of cocoa farmers, where children twelve years of age and sometimes younger were forced to do eighty to one hundred hours a week of hard manual labor on the cocoa plantations. They were paid nothing, fed little, and treated harshly. "The beatings were a part of my life," Aly Diabate told reporters. "Anytime they loaded you with bags [of cocoa beans] and you fell while carrying them, nobody helped you. Instead they beat you and beat you until you picked it up again."[9] Most of these children will never see their families again.

I can still taste the silky sweet taste of chocolate in my mouth. I double-check the glossy candy pouch, only to find again that it is empty. I scout around the desk in the hope of finding a morsel that has rolled away. Perhaps there is a piece of chocolate hiding under a stack of papers. I ruffle through the exams, but nothing is there.

On my desk, however, is British journalist Fred Pearce's *Confessions of an Eco-Sinner: Tracking Down the Sources of My Stuff*, in which he describes, among other things, his journey around the world to learn the origins of the food he eats. In Cameroon, he visits small farms that are an alternative to the large cocoa monoculture plantations.

A young boy who is the son of a subsistence cocoa farmer approaches him. "What," this child of a cocoa farmer asks, "does chocolate taste like?"

Dinner
John David is running in circles and wants me to chase him in a loop from the kitchen through the living room back into the kitchen. "Tag, Mama, you're it!"

He insists he is not hungry.

"You will be," I tell him.

"No, I won't."

I know from experience that soon he will be wanting something, and once the desire for food overcomes the desire for play, its demand will be immediate. I can certainly understand why parents resort to convenience foods. My son needs my attention after a long day at school, he will soon want food, and I am tired. The path of least resistance is to open the freezer door and pull out something that can be on the table more or less instantaneously with as little effort as possible. With the eye of someone whose distant ancestors could spot mushrooms camouflaged in the forest, I am searching for a bright red bag. Ah, there it is. "Chicken Breast NUGGETS," proclaims the thick plastic resealable family-pack bag. The bag crinkles as I tear it open. The directions on the back explain with pictograms and words that the nuggets will need to bake in a 425-degree oven for eleven to twelve minutes, which is, happily, just about exactly the same amount of time that the "french fry stix" in the purple plastic bag require.

I peer into the nugget bag. It has a pleasant smell, although it is not the smell of anything I recognize as chicken. If it were not for the bright yellow letters on the package identifying the contents as chicken breast, there would be little clue as to the identity of the contents inside. There are no feathers, no blood, no bones, no visible flesh. Just roundish flat pieces, the shape of a rock you might try to skip across a creek. The coated pieces are the golden color of fried food, speckled with little black dots. According to the fine print on the red package, the contents other than chicken consist of breader (bleached wheat four, salt, dextrose, yeast, soybean oil, spice, paprika) and batter (water, yellow corn flour, corn starch, [more] dextrose [i.e., corn fractions], salt, spices, sugar, autolyzed yeast extract [what is that?], modified food starch [how do you modify modified corn?], garlic powder, guar gum, and leavening [sodium acid pyrophosphate, sodium bicarbonate, monocalcium phosphate]). I break open a nugget and find flecked white matter inside. It is cold to the touch and has a solid texture. It gives no indication of being reconstituted anything.

I tear open the purple bag. The crinkly shaped potato sticks within are the same golden color as the fried and frozen chicken nuggets. They thawed a bit while I was examining the contents of the nugget bag and are now limp.

I pick up a handful and spread them onto a thin metal baking sheet beside the chicken nuggets, and they leave a residue of oil on my hands. Stepping carefully around my son's wooden blocks on the kitchen floor, I make my way to the oven and slip in the metal tray. In ten minutes the timer buzzes, and our dinner is ready.

The contents on the plate before me are various shades of brown. The appearance of the chicken nuggets has changed little in the baking. The french fry stix, which used to be predominantly light brown with dark ridges, are now predominantly dark brown, except for the smaller ones, which burned to a crisp in the 425-degree oven and are now pure black. If I did not have prior knowledge of the constituents of the items on my plate, would I have any idea what it is that I am about to eat? These breaded flat circular shapes and thin brown sticks bear no resemblance to any plant or animal.

John David slips off his chair before we have even finished praying.

"Where are you going?" I call after him. "You are not excused."

"Potty!" he calls back.

Oh.

I pick up a french fry and break it in half. It is a powdery white on the inside and oily (still) on the outside. It is crisp and warm, and just as I did at lunch, I reach for another before I have even finished chewing and swallowing the first. John David innocently plods back into the dining room with his pants around his ankles. "Wipe," he smiles up at me. "Peez [Please]."

When we return from the bathroom, John David uses a french fry to push his ketchup into a little hill. "Mama, yook [look], I made a volcano!"

I nibble at the breaded coating on the nugget. It smells fine and is not unpleasant to the taste. In preparation for writing this book, however, I have been reading about chickens, and what I have learned intrudes into the peace—or blessed disorder—of a family meal with a young child.

In the United States, I learned in one of the books that my husband, an ethicist, recommended to my attention, we eat more chicken than any other meat. This, write Peter Singer and Jim Mason in *The Ethics of What We Eat*, has not always been the case. Chicken was once more expensive than beef, but now it is cheaper, and consumption has doubled since 1970. Chicken meat has fallen in price through the poultry industry's effort to maximize efficiency and minimize cost in every aspect of production. In an economy where we once had cheap energy and where we still have an overabundance of No. 2 corn, this means centralizing broiler chicken production in large sheds that house thirty thousand or more birds and feeding them grain. Winged creatures that in my grandparents' day would have spent their days scampering on pasture and pecking grubs from the earth are now housed indoors in a cage that, according to trade association standards, should have ninety-six square inches per bird, which is about the size of the standard $8.5'' \times 11''$ sheet of paper on which my students print their essays. In this tight space, a mature chicken has such a limited range of movement that it is unable to stretch its wings or to move out of the territory of other aggressive birds.

To give broiler chickens more space would not be cost-effective. What is cost-effective is to breed them selectively for maximum meat production. According to *Poultry Science*, a trade journal, chickens today grow three times faster than chickens of the 1950s, while consuming only one-third as much food. Their bone structures, however, have not evolved at the same rate as their ability to convert grain to meat. Muscle and fat often outpace bone growth to such an extent that 90 percent of the birds have leg problems and 26 percent are in chronic pain as a result of bone disease.

Because of their confinement in large indoor sheds, they also suffer the consequences of breathing the fumes of their own excrement. In the right place in the right quantity, chicken droppings are a valuable soil fertilizer. Piled up under cages in industrial-size chicken sheds, the droppings emit ammonia, which burns the eyes and lungs of both human beings and caged birds. Concentrated in the air, ammonia causes respiratory disease, sores, breast blisters, and sometimes blindness. The poultry excrement also attracts flies and mice, which infest the homes of families in communities that neighbor the chicken pens.

A broiler chicken will typically live in a feeding pen for six weeks, at which point it is slaughtered. The sections of books that describe this process are often prefaced with warnings, such as "may be disturbing." Up to five birds at a time are taken by the legs and pushed, flapping and writhing, into cages for transport to the slaughterhouse, where their feet are snapped into metal shackles on a conveyor belt that will take them to the killing room. As they are carried upside down, their heads pass through an electrified bath that is intended to stun the birds so they will be unconscious when their throats are slit. According to Dr. Mohan Raj of the Department of Clinical Veterinary Science in Bristol, however, an electrical current strong enough to ensure that all the birds are unconscious would risk damage to the quality of the meat, so a weaker current is used, and "the majority of broilers are likely to be conscious and suffer pain and distress at slaughter."[10] With the pace of slaughter as high as 7,200 birds an hour, some birds on the conveyer belt will inevitably pass by the person slitting throats and are immersed alive into a tank of scalding water that will prepare the chickens for plucking. The nervous system of a chicken is very similar to our own. And the turnover rate of employees in some chicken slaughterhouses is over 100 percent.

"It is the hard and terrible truth that we live with," wrote the poet Mary Oliver, "feeding ourselves every day."[11]

2

eating in and out of eden

The need to feed ourselves daily is indeed a truth with which we live—but need it be so hard and terrible? According to the book of Acts, those baptized after Pentecost spent much time together in the temple and then "broke bread at home and ate their food with glad and generous hearts, praising God and having the goodwill of all the people" (Acts 2:46-47). My experience of eating in America, in contrast, is an experience of anxiety about the character of the food I am giving my child for breakfast. At lunch, I sit alone in a restaurant reading messages on disposable food wrappers, and for dinner I tear open plastic bags and dash reconstitued morsels of chicken into the oven. At some unspoken level, I move through the day with an emptiness that nothing has filled.

The Eucharist, the sacramental meal that is the well-spring of the Christian life, is an act of communion with God, other persons, and all creation, but my daily meals are typically eaten in ignorance of the lands and peoples that are the source of the food on my table. As a consumer in the global economy, my own life and that of my family is sustained by the soils of distant places and the labor of faceless others. When I try to peer beyond the attractive packaging of coffee, cereal, and frozen chicken nuggets to learn something about the origins of the food that I am feeding my family, I find barefoot children picking coffee beans, monocultures of crops dependent on petrochemical pesticides, and animals that have been mistreated.

I am not alone in feeling that something is amiss in the way we are eating in America. Kentucky author and farmer Wendell Berry has been writing for decades of the way in which our commodification of land and reduction of economic reason to mechanical models of efficiency have undone the personal relationships that once shaped our lives. The consequences of what he terms the "unsettling of America" include foreclosed family farms, decimated rural communities, and degraded ecosystems.[1] Soil scientist David Montgomery advises us that civilizations that erode soils eventually collapse, while journalists like Dale Pfeiffer and Paul Roberts caution that our globalized agricultural system, heavily dependent on fossil fuels for both the production and transportation of food, cannot be sustained.[2]

On the health front, Michael Pollan notes in *In Defense of Food* that humans in different climates and cultures have developed a wide diversity of dietary practices, most of which have served well the end of human well-being. In contrast, our Western fare of refined flours and sugars, highly processed foods, and large portions of meat has contributed to our high rates of diabetes, obesity, cardiovascular disease, and diet-related cancers. An American child of European descent born in the year 2000 has a one in three chance of developing type 2 diabetes, and the risks to an African American or Hispanic child are even greater. Two-thirds of all Americans are overweight or obese.[3] Witnessing our national disavowal first of fats and then of carbohydrates as we ride the wave of one dietary trend after another, Pollan comments that we suffer from "the lack of a steadying culture of food" that the accumulated wisdom of human experience should provide.[4]

Barbara Kingsolver shares Pollan's diagnosis of the weakness of our national culture of eating and drinking. In the United States, she writes, "we have yet to come up with a strong set of generalized norms, passed down through families, for savoring and sensibly consuming what our land and climate can give us. We have, instead a string of fad diets . . . and we long for a Food Leviticus to save us from the sinful roil of cheap fats and carbs."[5] Our ways with food are serving us poorly, but they are so deeply entrenched that "it can take something on the order of religion to invoke new, more conscious behaviors."[6]

> "We long for a Food Leviticus to save us from the sinful roil of cheap fats and carbs."

For some, the Food Leviticus has come in the form of a variety of Christian diet programs. In "The Promised Land of Weight Loss," R. Marie Griffith catalogs a long series of faith-based diet books, starting with Presbyterian minister Charlie W. Shed's 1957 book *Pray Your Weight Away*. This has been followed by a variety of popular titles, including Victor Kane's *Devotions for Dieters* (1973), Patricia Kreml's *Slim for Him* (1978), and Gwen Shamblin's *The Weigh Down Diet* (1997). Dieters have found support in groups such as Believercise, Faithfully Fit, and Jesus Is the Weigh. Griffith comments that some of us may chortle at book titles like C. S. Lovett's *Help Lord—The Devil Wants Me Fat!* (1977), but she emphasizes that "hundreds of thousands of downhearted dieters look to this kind of devotional advice for redemption as assiduously as they have ever listened

to Sunday sermons, and often with a great deal more desperation."[7] Griffith urges empathy with those whose voices
speak to us in this literature: men and women like Joan
Cavanaugh, who writes in *More of Jesus, Less of Me* that
she was mercilessly ridiculed as a child and took solace in
the "altar" of the cookie cupboard. Christian churches can
be places of compassionate support for people struggling
with weight issues and the estimated ten million American
women and one million American men engaged in a life-
and-death struggle with eating disorders.[8]

Beyond support for persons struggling with diets or
eating disorders, Christianity offers a theological vision
that can contribute to a renewed culture of eating and
drinking in America. Our tradition testifies that we are
not ultimately consumers in the globalized economy but
human persons created with a vocation to live in communion with God, one another, and all of creation. This
communion is characterized by reverence for God and life-
giving relationships of mutual charity and care amongst
humans and between human persons and all of creation.
Eating and drinking can be consumptive acts that violate
covenantal relationships or sacramental events that sig-
nify and embody communion. In this chapter, I will high-
light aspects of the biblical narrative that contribute to the
Christian sacramental vision. The scriptures open to us a
vision of an Edenic communion marred by human transgression and redeemed by the grace of covenant and the
inbreaking of the reign of God in Christ.

Edenic Communion

"The eye and the mind," wrote Ephrem the Syrian (ca.
306–379 c.e.), "traveled over the lines [of Scripture] as

over a bridge, and entered together the story of Paradise."[9] There, Ephrem's poem continues, he beheld "the bowers of the righteous dripping with unguents and fragrant with scents, garlanded with fruits, crowned with blossoms. . . . [Paradise] delighted me as much by its peacefulness as by its beauty: in it there resides a beauty that has no spot; in it exists a peacefulness that knows no fear."[10]

When artist Thomas Cole crossed over his own bridge into Eden, he painted a lush and verdant scene. In *The Garden of Eden* (1828), arching trees frame the view of a distant mountain from which pure white water cascades into a glistening lake. In the foreground, the waters of a creek glide over red, purple, and blue gemstones, and butterflies feed on the nectar of the iris, phlox, daises, and columbine that flourish beside the stream. The trees that reach to the blue sky on the right and left sides of the horizon are a mixture of tropical palms and deciduous species, and clusters of bananas and ripe red berries hang from some of their branches. A bird of paradise with blue and red feathers perches on a branch above a shaded pool, and a pair of white swans glides effortlessly on its surface. In the central area of the painting is an open meadow dotted with flowers, and on the left side of the meadow a human couple raises their arms in exultation to the light that streams from above. Across the meadow stands a stag, a traditional symbol of longing for God. "The scene," Cole writes in his sketch book, "as it exists in my mind's eye, is very beautiful . . . much more beautiful, I know, than my art can realize."[11]

The story of a peaceable creation in Genesis 1:1—2:3 that inspired Cole's art and Ephrem's poetry comes from the sixth century B.C.E., a period when the people of Israel lived in exile and servitude in Babylon. Like Ephrem, they crossed a bridge to enter the revelatory vision of a beautiful world without fear. Each year, their Babylonian overlords celebrated an annual festival in which they recounted the story of their chief god Marduk, who made the earth and the vaults of heaven by slaying the body of the goddess Tiamat and dividing her carcass in two. In Genesis 1, in contrast, creation originates not with violence but with the power of God's word: "Then God said, 'Let there be . . .'" (Genesis 1:3). And there *was* light, water, sky, earth, vegetation, seed, and fruit. God creates, according to Christian interpretations of Genesis, *ex nihilo* and *ex amore*: out of nothing and out of freely overflowing love, out of sheer desire to share divine life with that which is not God.

Creation enacted in the power of the divine *logos* (John 1:1-3) is carefully ordered: sky, water, and land are each differentiated and gifted with forms of life appropriate to their domains. Great lights and winged birds grace the dome of the sky, swarming creatures glide through the waters of the deep, and living creatures are given the blessing to "be fruitful and multiply" (Genesis 1:22). On the sixth day of creation, God made humankind in the divine image, male and female. To a degree unique among all creatures, the human person participates in God's love and *logos* through our capacity for self-transcending communion and compassion, our ability to reason, and our freedom for virtuous action. Like the kings that people of the ancient cultures of Mesopotamia believed to represent their deities, human persons are given dominion over creation (Genesis 1:28) and entrusted to govern in a manner reflective of the character of God. The first human person, wrote Gregory of Nyssa (ca. 335–384), bore a scepter of immortality and was clothed not in purple robes but in virtue, "the most royal of all raiment."[12]

Eating was part of the primordial goodness of creation. The human person, Gregory of Nyssa continues, was brought as a guest into the house of creation after the divine host "had decked the habitation with beauties of every kind, and prepared this great and varied banquet," assigning to us "not the acquiring of what was not there, but the enjoyment of the things which were there."[13] Given for our enjoyment were "every plant yielding seed that is upon the face of all the earth, and every tree with seed in its fruit" (Genesis 1:29). Like the beasts of the earth, the birds of the air, and the creatures that creep on the ground—all of whom are given green plants for food (Genesis 1:30)—the original human person was an herbivore. Eating in Eden was a bloodless communion in which all creatures lived peaceably without taking life from another. "God saw everything that he had made, and indeed, it was very good" (Genesis 1:31). Beholding this vision, Ephrem writes, "I gave praise as far as I was able."[14]

The account of creation in Genesis 1:1—2:3 is followed by a second narrative of human origins that biblical scholars trace to the ninth century B.C.E. In this story, humanity is created prior to the plants and animals as an earth creature (*adam*) made out of the earth (*adamah*) into which God blows the breath of life (Genesis 2:7). Out of this same earth, God "made to grow every tree that is pleasant to the sight and good for food" (Genesis 2:9), and from this earth animals are formed. When no animal of the field or bird of the air suffices to provide a suitable companion for *adam*, God causes a deep sleep to fall upon the earth creature and then fashions from one of *adam*'s rib a partner, differentiating *adam* into man (*ish*) and woman (*ishshah*). "This at last," says *adam*, "is bone of my bones and flesh of my flesh" (Genesis 2:23). Although *ish* and *ishshah* share a unique bond, their communion with trees and animals and birds is evident in that all are fashioned by God from the same earth. God places the man and the woman in the garden of Eden to till it and to keep it (Genesis 2:15). *Abad,* the Hebrew word translated "to keep," is also used in reference to the worship of God (Exodus 4:23). In Eden, humans are both the farmers and priests of creation.

In this second creation narrative, as in the story that opens the book of Genesis, the human person is an herbivore. "And the LORD God commanded [*adam*], 'You may freely eat of every tree of the garden'" (Genesis 2:16). In the varied fruit of every diverse species of tree, John of Damascus (ca. 676–749) comments, God invites us to taste the invisible divine power through which the great diversity of all visible things are made (Romans 1:20): "Through all things ascend to me the Creator; from every tree harvest one fruit, namely me who am the life. Let all things bear the fruit of life for you: make participation in me the stuff of your own existence."[15] In Eden we lived free of anxiety with but one responsibility: "to sing as do the angels, without ceasing or intermission, the praises of the Creator, and to delight in contemplation of Him."[16]

Human Transgression

In the middle of the garden stood one tree that the man and the woman were not to touch. "You may freely eat of every tree of the garden," God told *adam*, the earth creature, "but of the tree of the knowledge of good and evil you shall not eat, for in the day that you eat of it, you shall die" (Genesis 2:16-17). This commandment, explains Irenaeus, the second-century bishop of Gaul, is both a testimony to the reality of human freedom and a humbling reminder that despite this freedom we remain creatures of the earth.[17]

The serpent offered Adam and Eve a different interpretation of God's command.

"You will not die [if you eat of the tree]," said the serpent, "for God knows that when you eat of it your eyes will be opened, and you will be like God, knowing good and evil" (Genesis 3:4-5).

German theologian Eugen Drewermann believes that these simple words changed Adam and Eve's experience of Paradise. Eden had been a place in which they delighted in the goodness of God's creation, a garden of perfect harmony and trust. Now, this trust was called into question.[18] "Are the words of the serpent true?" they surely wondered. "Did God indeed mislead us? Is the serpent untrustworthy? Or is it God who is not to be trusted? Are we creatures among untrustworthy creatures, or children of an untrustworthy God?" These questions sowed fears and insecurities. Troubled by these thoughts and perhaps desiring some comfort or reassurance, Eve reached out to pluck something to eat.

"So when the woman saw that the tree was good for food, and that it was a delight to the eyes, and that the tree was to be desired to make one wise, she took of its fruit and ate; and she also gave some to her husband, who was with her, and he ate" (Genesis 3:6). The fruit through which human sin entered the world was not spoiled, rotten, or ridden with worms. To the contrary, it was delightful and attractive, and the serpent described it as a food with the power to grant participation in divinity.

Augustine, the fourth-century bishop of Hippo, identified the underlying cause of human transgression as *superbia*, a Latin word that is imprecisely translated into English as "pride." Pride, in Augustine's sense of the term, is not a matter of esteem for one's own accomplishments, nor even an inordinate sense of self-importance. *Superbia* has the precise theological meaning of displacing the Creator with a creature and thereby unraveling the entire order of the cosmos. In the Genesis story, it is explicitly stated that Eve and Adam eat the forbidden fruit with the enticement of the serpent's promise that "they will become like God." They violated their communion with God both by breaking a divine commandment and by eating with the intention of grasping for themselves qualities of divinity that can only be bequeathed as gift.

More commonly, the *superbia* that underlies our acts of transgression is more subtle, as Augustine describes in his *Confessions*. Reflecting on the expanse of his life from infancy onward, Augustine describes his own experience with a fruit tree in a garden. One night, at the age of sixteen, Augustine and a group of his friends shook the fruit from a pear tree near his family's vineyard. They ate a few pieces of fruit and then carried off a huge load of pears to throw to some pigs. Scrutinizing the multiple layers of his own motivations, Augustine writes that he did not really desire the fruit itself, as he had ample pears of better quality in his own home. What he did desire was the friendship of the other boys, and he took pleasure in doing together with them something that was forbidden. The friendship that he desired was itself a good of God's creation. His sin, he explains, was not his love of friendship, but its disordered character; he delighted in friendship more than in God, who has written in both the law of Moses (Exodus 20:15) and the law of the human heart (Romans 2:14) that one shall not steal. Human friendship is "a nest of love and gentleness because of the unity it brings about between many souls. Yet sin is committed for the sake of all these things and others of this kind when, in consequence of an immoderate urge towards those things which are at the bottom end of the scale of good, we abandon the higher and supreme goods, that is you, Lord God, and your truth and your law (Psalm 118:142). These inferior goods have their delights, but not comparable to my God who has made them all."[19] We transgress not because we desire things that are evil, but because our desire for lesser goods eclipses our desire for God.

Adam and Eve ate of the fruit of the tree in the middle of the garden, and "the eyes of both were opened, and they knew that they were naked; and they sewed fig leaves together and made loincloths for themselves" (Genesis 3:7). The Hebrew verb "to know" (*yada*) can have sexual connotations, as it surely does in this account of the act of eating of the tree of the knowledge of good and evil. The knowledge that Adam and Eve acquired included the knowledge that humans are sexual beings, and our sexual nature and physical hungers are deeply intertwined. Eating and sexual intercourse can both be acts of profound human communion; a family gathered at table all take into their bodies portions of the same one bread, and husband and wife "become one flesh" (Genesis 2:24). But eating and intercourse become grave violations of communion when they are acts of consumption, gluttony, domination, or lust. After we have eaten with Adam and Eve of the fruit of the forbidden tree, Elizabeth Theokritoff comments, "the world around us is no longer a revelation of our Creator, but a resource to satisfy our appetites."[20]

A creature that approaches creation as a consumable resource for the satisfaction of appetites must be kept at a distance from the tree of eternal life that Ephrem envisioned growing on the heights of the mountain of Paradise. And so God sent *adam* "forth from the garden of Eden, to till the ground from which he was taken. He drove out the man; and at the east of the garden of Eden he placed the cherubim, and a sword flaming and turning to guard the way to the tree of life" (Genesis 3:23-24).

Adam and Eve took leave of the garden where tree branches hung heavy with succulent fruit and beasts ate peacefully of green plants, and they entered a land that was dry and sparsely vegetated. The ground that they tilled was the same *adamah* from which they themselves had been fashioned. But in the breach of communion with God, the relationships at all levels of human existence became disordered and devolved into violence and death. Adam and Eve bore two sons, and Cain murdered his brother and spilled his blood upon the ground (Genesis 4:1-16). Cain's descendents fashioned human culture and civilization—lyres and pipes, tools, and tents—a civilization that practiced seventy-sevenfold vengeance for acts of injury (Genesis 4:24). As the human generations multiplied—through Seth, Enosh, Kenan, Mahalalel, Jared, Enoch, Methuselah, and Lamesh—so, too, did the corruption of creation. Even the boundaries of heaven and earth were breached when divine beings in the heavenly court took for themselves fair daughters of humankind (Genesis 6:1-2). "The LORD saw that the wickedness of humankind was great in the earth, and that every inclination of the thoughts of their hearts was only evil continually. And the Lord was sorry that he had made humankind on the earth, and it grieved him to his heart" (Genesis 6:5-6).

Covenant

The grief of God is an expression of what Rabbi Abraham Joshua Heschel terms "the divine *pathos*," the passionate concern of God for creation. The God of the Bible, he emphasizes, is not the "unmoved mover" of Aristotle but a God who is both wholly other than creation and wholly bound to creation in love. Scripture attests to a "God in search of man," a God brokenhearted by the corruption of creation and in need of human righteousness to help bring about creation's repair.[21] In the covenant narratives of Noah and Naamah, Abraham and Sarah, the wilderness sojourn, the giving of Torah on Sinai, and the temple meals, we find wisdom about eating and drinking.

The Noahide Covenant: Eating With Reverence for Life. The God in search of human hearts found righteousness and goodness in the persons of Noah and Naamah who "walked with God" (Genesis 6:9). "I will establish my covenant with you," said God, instructing Noah to build an ark of cypress wood in preparation for a flood that would inundate the earth (Genesis 6:18). In the face of this impending destruction, the covenant is a relationship of commitment to the preservation of the great diversity of life. God instructed Noah to take into the ark male and female of every kind of bird, animal, and creeping thing in order "to keep them alive. Also take with you every kind of food that is eaten, and store it up; and it shall serve as food for you and for them" (Genesis 6:20-21). To Naamah, God said, "Walk across the land and gather the seeds of all the flowers and all the trees. Take two of every kind of living plant and bring each one into the ark. They shall not be for food, but they shall be your garden, to tend and to keep."[22]

Noah sheltered pairs of every kind of living creature in the decks of the ark and gathered into its store-holds every kind of food that is eaten, including vine shoots for new vine plantings, fig saplings, and young olive trees. Naamah gathered the cones of redwoods, the nuts of cypress and cedar, the seeds of every kind of flower, and spores from the moss that carpets the forest floor. For forty days and nights, Noah and Naamah and their children worked day and night to feed the creatures entrusted to their care. They had tree branches for the elephants, *chatsubah* (foraging plants) for the deer, and *z'khukhit* for the ostriches. "We had much trouble in the ark," Noah's son Shem later told Abraham's servant Eliezer. "The animals which usually feed by day we fed by day, and those which normally feed at night we fed by night."[23] Once, when Noah was late in feeding the lion, it bit him, and he went away limping. "Why is Noah called righteous?" one rabbi asks another. "Because," the other replies, "he fed the creatures of the Holy One, and became like his Creator."[24]

When the waters of the flood subsided, the weary refugees disembarked onto dry ground, and Noah built an altar to the Lord. "As for me," God said, "I am establishing my covenant with you and your descendants after you, and with every living creature that is with you, the birds, the domestic animals, and every animal of the earth with you, as many as came out of the ark" (Genesis 9:8-10). This troth is known as the Noahide covenant, and it is inclusive of all living creatures. According to Rabbinic tradition, it holds all the descendants of Noah and Naamah responsible for adherence to seven basic commandments, six of which had already been given in Eden. Those six laws forbade blasphemy, idolatry, grave sexual immorality, murder, and theft, and called for the establishment of courts of justice. The additional seventh law is given in the post-diluvian world as a concession to the imperfect character of our existence east of Eden. God renews the blessings of fecundity bestowed on the original creation (Genesis 8:17; 9:1), but God also tells Noah and his sons, "The fear and dread of you shall rest on every animal of the earth, and on every bird of the air, on everything that creeps on the ground, and on all the fish of the sea, into your hand they are delivered. Every moving thing that lives shall be food for you; and just as I gave you the green plants, I give you everything. Only you shall not eat flesh with its life, that is, its blood" (Genesis 9:2-4). The blood of an animal, its life-force, must be returned to God.

This prescription, explains biblical scholar Jacob Milgrom, is not a primitive taboo that infiltrated ancient Israel; there is no evidence of this practice in any other culture of the ancient Near East. Rather, this is an intentional innovation rooted in a fundamental theological principle: "Life is inviolable; it may not be treated lightly. [Human] kind has a right to nourishment, not to life."[25] Although God concedes to humanity the right to eat animal flesh in our exile from the peaceable kingdom of Eden, God also establishes a dietary discipline intended to curb our violent nature and embody a fundamental principle of covenantal eating and drinking: reverence for God, the Creator of life.

Sarah and Abraham: Extending Hospitality to Strangers. According to the Rabbis, all humans who observe the Noahide commandments are children of Noah, righteous Gentiles who will share in the world to come. At the same time, the God of divine *pathos* seeks to deepen the covenant relationship, and the human person continues to hunger for the holy. Ten generations after Noah, God chose Abraham "that he may charge his children and his household after him to keep the way of the LORD by doing righteousness and justice" (Genesis 18:19). God spoke to Abraham of a covenant that would endure from generation to generation, marked with the sign of circumcision of the foreskin of male flesh. Abraham, in turn, "fell on his face and laughed" (Genesis 17:17). He was one hundred years old and his wife was ninety. His only son Ishmael had been born to Hagar, an Egyptian slave-girl, because Sarah was barren.

One day, as Abraham sat at the entrance of his tent, three strangers appeared. Abraham ran to meet them, bowed down to the ground, and invited them to rest beneath the shade of the oaks of Mamre. He instructed Sarah to make cakes with three measures of choice flour, and he hastened to the pasture to select a tender calf. As the guests reclined, Abraham served them curds, milk, the flesh of the calf, and the bread that Sarah had prepared. One of the visitors promised to return in due season, at which time Sarah would have a son. Sarah, who had been listening at the door of the tent, laughed to herself. Neither she nor Abraham realized that the strangers they had received were in fact the Lord and two angels, and, indeed, it came to pass that Sarah did conceive and bear a son. She suckled Isaac lovingly, and he fell asleep in her arms. "God has brought laughter for me," Sarah said. "Everyone who hears will laugh with me. Who would ever have said to Abraham that Sarah would nurse children?" (Genesis 21:6-7) God's covenant promise would have been barren, were it not for food shared with strangers in the act of hospitality.

Food in the Wilderness: Divine Gifts and Human Cravings. The God of *pathos* cares for the people of the covenant like a nursing mother who comforts her child (Isaiah 66:13), and food and drink are a primary expression of this maternal love. The biblical stories of Abraham and Sarah and their descendents come from a region of the ancient Near East where famine was a periodic reality, caused by lack of rainfall or degraded soils or warfare and siege. Famine takes Abraham and Sarah to Egypt in search of food (Genesis 12:10), and the sons of Jacob journey to the Nile delta in search of grain, only to discover that it is their own brother, Joseph, who has become governor of Egypt after advising the pharaoh that his dreams were a portent of a coming famine (Genesis 37–45). When Jacob's descendants are enslaved by a subsequent pharaoh who did not know Joseph, God has compassion for the misery of the people. "Indeed," God tells Moses, "I know their sufferings, and I have come down to deliver them from the Egyptians, and to bring them up out of that land to a good and broad land, a land flowing with milk and honey" (Exodus 3:7-8).

As the people of Israel sojourn through the wilderness after fleeing Egypt on the night of Passover, they complain of their hunger and thirst. "I am going to rain bread from heaven for you," God assures Moses, and in the morning the Israelites awake to find beneath the morning dew a flakey white wafer that tasted like honey (Exodus 16:4), perhaps the honey-dew excretions of insects that feed on the twigs of the tamarisk tree. Moses instructed them to gather only enough of this manna for their own need, one *omer* for each person of each tent. "Eating," comments Ellen Davis, "is the most basic of all cultural and economic acts," and Israel's response to the gift of manna is a litmus test of their separation from the culture of Egypt, where the pharaoh appropriated up to half the harvest of grain for the royal granaries.[26] Is food a commodity to be used in the service of imperial power or a gift and sign of God's presence? Some of the Israelites gathered more manna than Moses had instructed and some gathered less, but when it came time to measure the sweet wafers with the *omer*, each had as much as was needed (Exodus 16:17-18; cf. 2 Corinthians 8:13-15).

Many of the Israelites, however, were unsatisfied. "If only we had meat to eat!" a rabble wailed. "We remember the fish we used to eat in Egypt for nothing, the cucumbers, the melons, the leeks, the onions, and the garlic; but now our strength is dried up, and there is nothing at all but this manna to look at" (Numbers 11:4-6). Frustrated almost to the point of despair, Moses cried out to God, "I am not able to carry all this people alone" (Numbers 11:14). Then, a gale of wind arose from the Gulf of Aqaba carrying quails so numerous they fell in piles two cubits deep. The Israelites worked all day, through the night, and into the next day gathering the quail, and no one had less than ten *omers*. The divine *pathos*, Heschel emphasizes, is a *pathos* with an *ethos* (ethic), and when humans violate this ethic we experience God's *pathos* as anger.[27] Those Israelites who bit into the flesh of the quail were stricken with a plague, and the place was called *Kibroth-hattaavah* because there they buried the people who had the craving (Numbers 11:34).

Torah Practices for Eating as a Holy People. On the third new moon after the Israelite's departure from Pharaoh, the people of Israel and their caravan of cattle, goats, and sheep entered the desert of Sinai. They set camp, and the Lord instructed Moses to keep all the men pure for three days and to set firm boundaries around the mountain that no person or animal would trespass. On the third day, they awoke to the sound of thunder and lightning. "Awe," Heschel emphasizes, "precedes faith; it is at the root of faith."[28] Had the people of Israel received the torah without the awe of God, they would have been like a treasurer given a key to an inner chamber with no key to the outer door.

Moses ascended the heights of Mount Sinai shrouded in smoke and received from God the Torah. This Hebrew word is often translated into English as "law," but *torah* is better rendered as teaching, a practical wisdom that enables one to walk in the ways of God. God's intent on Sinai is to form a covenant that will make of Israel "a priestly kingdom and a holy nation" (Exodus 19:6). According to Rabbinic tradition, Israel is chosen not because God's love is exclusive but because other peoples of the earth refused the gift of *torah* that was offered also to them. "There is an eternal cry in the world," writes Heschel. "*God is beseeching man* to answer, to return."[29] God seeks a communion of action with humanity in which our deeds and our paths disclose divine intentions. "The *torah* is primarily *divine ways* rather than *divine laws*," an invitation to holiness in which God invites Israel to "do what he is."[30]

In our imperfect world east of Eden, the torah cannot come in pure form. Just as humanity is in exile from the garden of Paradise, writes Heschel, so too the torah is in exile. God clothed Adam and Eve in garments before their departure from Eden, and the glory of the Lord is clothed in a rough garment like burlap and appears to us in a form accommodated to our exilic state. The burlap coverings of the Torah include passages that are inconsistent with the spirit of God and discussions of murders and wars. In the messianic era, the pure form of the *torah* will be revealed. In the interim, a people in exile from Eden must discern the wisdom that the garments clothe.[31]

"The earth is the LORD's, and all that is in it" (Psalm 24:1). This theological principle is at the heart of the teaching of the covenant. The land is not a commodity to be bought or sold. The earth belongs to God and is shared with humans as a blessing that we are to cherish wisely. "When you enter the land that I am giving you," the Lord said to Moses, "the land shall observe a sabbath for the LORD. Six years you shall sow your field, and six years you shall prune your vineyard, and gather in their yield; but in the seventh year there shall be a sabbath of complete rest for the land, a sabbath for the LORD" (Leviticus 25:2-4). Biblical scholar Jacob Milgrom cites evidence from the first-century Jewish scholar Philo of Alexandria and the historian Josephus that the Sabbath rest was observed regularly, and that these periods of abstention from agricultural usage contributed to the sustenance of the fertility of the land.[32]

The blessings of fertility were to be shared by all. Just as God acted with justice and compassion for the people of Israel in their enslavement to Pharaoh, so too Israel must act with justice and compassion for the widow, the orphan, the neighbor, and the strangers in their midst (Deuteronomy 10:17-19). "If there is among you anyone in need . . . do not be hard-hearted or tight-fisted toward your needy neighbor. You should rather open your hand, willingly lending enough to meet the need, whatever it may be" (Deuteronomy 15:7-8). The Israelites were instructed not to reap their vineyards bare nor harvest to the very edges of the field, but to leave something for the poor and the alien to glean (Leviticus 19:9-10; 23:22; Deuteronomy 24:19-20; Ruth 2:1-3). Grain, grapes, or olives that grew of their own accord during the Sabbath year were to be left for the poor and the wild animals to eat (Exodus 23:10-11). Every third year a full tithe of the produce of the land was to be reserved for the Levites, the resident aliens, the orphans, and the widows, that they "may come and eat their fill so that the LORD your God may bless you" (Deuteronomy 14:29). In an agrarian economy where a poor harvest could necessitate indebtedness to others that could eventually lead to loss of the land to a debtor, the Torah calls for a Jubilee year of redemption every fiftieth year, at which time all land would return to the family that was its original steward (Lev. 25:8-10).

The Torah also includes very specific dietary guide-lines. Leviticus, Davis comments, recognizes "eating as *the* definitive cultural act."[33] It is an act, Milgrom emphasizes, central to God's invitation to holiness. If one surveys the Pentateuch, he explains, one will find that the passages in which God enjoins Israel to holiness are concentrated in teachings on idolatry, the priesthood, and the dietary laws (Leviticus 11:1-47; Deuteronomy 14:4-21). For the people of Israel, the dietary disciplines are the daily practices that serve as "rungs on the ladder of holiness, leading to a life of pure thought and deed, characteristic of the nature of God."[34] These disciplines place no restrictions on eating foods from the vegetable and fruit kingdoms but severely limit the choice of animal foods to several domesticated herbivorous species: cattle, sheep, and goats. The meat of these animals is not to be eaten with milk, as it would vio-late life to "boil a kid in its mother's milk" (Exodus 23:19; 34:26; Deuteronomy 14:21). Several kinds of fish, pigeons, turtledoves, several kinds of nonraptorial birds, and locusts are also permitted; however, even the permissible animals and birds may only be eaten if they are slaughtered by someone with the spiritual and practical training to render death in the most painless way possible and return the blood of the animal to God.[35] Any other form of consumption of flesh is impure. In Leviticus, Milgrom explains, impurity is associated with death, and purity with the holiness of the God of life. God's injunction "You shall be holy, for I the Lord your God am holy" (Leviticus 19:2) is an invitation to live with an ever deeper reverence for God, the source of all life.[36]

Temple Meals: Eating in Communion with God. The Torah the Israelites received from God included instructions for the construction of a tabernacle, a portable sanctuary carried through the wilderness and then into the land of Canaan. The tabernacle was made with the skilled craftsmanship of the people and their finest gold, silver, and bronze; blue and crimson yarns; fine purple linens; acacia wood; and soft leather. Veiled behind an inner curtain was an ark of wood inlaid in gold that bore the tablets of the law. Outside the curtain stood an altar and table framed of acacia wood and adorned with gold molding and trim. On this table, the Lord said to Moses, "You shall set the bread of the Presence . . . before me always" (Exodus 25:30).

It was a common practice of other ancient Mesopotamian religions to display bread before a deity. Nonetheless, explains Milgrom, there is a wide gulf between the bread rites of the Egyptians and Hittites and those of ancient Israel. Whereas others baked bread for their gods daily, Israel prepared bread weekly as a token offering whose purpose was symbolic exposure, not food.[37] The bread was a tangible reminder of the covenant, a relationship that entailed both the sustaining divine presence and human responsibility.

The rituals of the tabernacle and its priesthood are central to this covenant relationship. Torah in the form of words alone, Milgrom emphasizes, dissipates into the air, but participatory rituals enact and embody the covenant teachings and embed them in the memory of the people.[38] When Solomon built the temple in Jerusalem in the tenth century B.C.E., it became the focal point of the religious life of the people of Israel, who were instructed by Moses to return to God the first portion of the bounty of the "land with flowing streams, with springs and underground waters welling up in valleys and hills, a land of wheat and barley, of vines and fig trees and pomegranates, a land of olive trees and honey, a land where you may eat bread without scarcity" (Deuteronomy 8:7-9). Pilgrims sojourned to the temple at three pivotal points in the agricultural year: the Feast of Tabernacles, celebrated on the first full moon after the autumnal equinox in October that marked the beginning of the rainy season; Passover, celebrated on the first full moon after the vernal equinox at the time of the spring harvest; and, fifty days later, the Feast of Firstfruits. Pilgrims entering the temple heard the psalmody of the Levites and beheld the priests officiating at the sacrifices to which they contributed their own offerings of new grain, lambs, bulls, rams, and goats. Animals were sacrificed in the most painless way possible by cutting the arteries in their necks, and the blood that gushed into a bowl was sprinkled on the altar. The smoke of the burning sacrifice that wafted upward was a symbol of the life of the covenant relation and the sacrificial atonement for sin.

"If I were hungry," God declares through the psalmist, "I would not tell you, for the world and all that is in it is mine. Do I eat the flesh of bulls, or drink the blood of goats?" (Psalm 50:12-13). The intent of temple sacrifice was not to feed God but "to bring near," as the Hebrew word *korban* implies, and "to make sacred," as the Latin root of the word "sacrifice" suggests. The act, Milgrom explains, is an act of transference of something from the common to the sacred realm, "making it a gift for God."[39] In the festivals that marked the rhythm of the agricultural year, a portion of the grain, wine, and animals that nourished the life of the people of Israel were given to God, the source of all life, and the priests and the pilgrims ate of these same offerings. "Life was shared in communion with God," comments Jacob Neusner, "humanity and God sustained in the same way."[40]

The Inbreaking of the Reign of God

Those who served as the final editors of the books of the Hebrew Scriptures were self-critical about the life of their own people. The story of Israel is recounted as a story of holiness and sin, homecoming and exile, sovereignty and subjection to the empires of Babylonia, Assyria, Antiochus Epiphanes, and Julius Caesar. In the eighth century B.C.E., at a time when some members of the people of Israel feasted while orphans were abandoned, the prophet Isaiah lamented the iniquities of his people and the faithlessness of a king who had made a military alliance with Assyria. The prophet, writes Heschel, feels deeply the divine *pathos* and "is convulsed by it to the depths of his soul."[41]

Isaiah spoke not only the *pathos* of grief but also the promise of the coming of one anointed by the Spirit of the Lord who will judge the poor with righteousness and act with equity for the meek (Isaiah 11:1-4). The prophet envisioned a restoration of the peaceable kingdom of Eden where the wolf will lie down with the lamb, and the calf with the lion—a world in which "they will not hurt or destroy on all my holy mountain; for the earth will be full of the knowledge of the LORD as the waters cover the sea" (Isaiah 11:9). Upon the holy mountain, "the LORD of hosts will make for all peoples a feast of rich food, a feast of well-aged wines, of rich food filled with marrow, of well-aged wines strained clear. And he will destroy on this mountain the shroud that is cast over all peoples, the sheet that is spread over all nations; he will swallow up death forever" (Isaiah 25:6-8).

At the dawn of the first century c.e., the people of Israel longed for the coming of God's messiah as they struggled under the dominion of the empire of Caesar Augustus. In Nazareth and the other small villages of the region, the women who gathered daily in the courtyards between their homes to grind grain into flour may well have dreamed or talked of the coming of God's reign. Their word for "food," *lechem,* was also the word for "bread," the primary staple of their diet. They mixed the coarse flour of wheat or barley with water, kneaded it into dough, and baked round loaves in a wood- or charcoal-burning oven. The bread could be served with olives or olive oil, figs, or perhaps some goat cheese.

The common people lived on the narrow margin between a simple fare of bread and water and the lurking reality of hunger. A drought or blight could leave villagers with empty earthen storage jars. In the days of Caesar and the Jewish rulers whom he appointed to govern the provinces, subsistence was threatened not only by the variability of the weather but also by imperial decree. King Herod (40—4 B.C.E.), governor of Judea, exacted heavy taxes to support the construction of a more grandiose temple, a new capital city, and other projects. Village land could be subject to a tax of as much as 50 percent of its yield, above and beyond the required temple tithe. If poor harvests or taxation left a family in need, they could borrow money from members of a small patronage class, often at a very high rate of interest. If they could not repay the loan, the land they had worked would be lost, and they would become tenant farmers on the estates of others, or sojourners in the city in search of wage labor. The Kinneret Boat, a first-century hull excavated from the Sea of Galilee in 1986, testifies to the struggle of the life of the people. The fishing boat was cobbled together from twelve different kinds of wood salvaged from weathered vessels, a combination of fine craftsmanship and poor materials. Fishermen like Simon and Andrew, speculates biblical scholar John Crossan, may have garnered a large catch but were then required to sell their fish on the terms of Herod Antipas, who opened the new capital city of Tiberias on the shore of the Sea of Galilee in 20 C.E. and likely instituted taxes on nets, boats, and fishing rights.[42]

It was in the days of Caesar and Herod the Great that the angel Gabriel appeared to Mary and announced that she would give birth to a son, Jesus, who "will reign over the house of Jacob forever, and of his kingdom there will be no end" (Luke 1:30-33). Gabriel reassured the doubts and fears of Mary, who was a virgin, and she sojourned to visit her cousin Elizabeth, who was also with child. When Elizabeth gave Mary her blessing, Mary's spirit rejoiced and magnified the Lord: "He has brought down the powerful from their thrones, and lifted up the lowly; he has filled the hungry with good things, and sent the rich away empty" (Luke 1:52-53).

The God of the people Israel is a God of divine *pathos*, and Jesus Christ, in the words of theologian Monika Hellwig, is "the compassion of God."[43] The child born of Mary's womb and anointed by the Holy Spirit in the waters of the River Jordan is both the incarnate *logos* of God (John 1:4) and a human being who knows the fear of famine and the reality of thirst. Following his baptism, Jesus went forth into the wilderness, where he fasted forty days and forty nights "and afterwards he was famished" (Matthew 4:2). Jesus Christ "was baptized as man," wrote Gregory Nazianzus in the fourth century, "but he remitted sins as God. . . . He hungered—but he fed thousands; yea, he is the Bread that giveth life, and that is of heaven. He thirsted—but he cried, if any man thirst, let him come unto me and drink. Yea, he promised that fountains should flow from them that believe."[44] Christ is both the visible image of the invisible God (2 Corinthians 4:4) and a vulnerable human being.

"Yeshua" is the title of a portrait of Jesus by Peter De Firis awarded second place in "Jesus 2000," a contest soliciting depictions of Jesus Christ for the new millennium. This portrayal of a Semitic Jesus is a reminder that Jesus was a Jew in a Jewish Palestine controlled by Rome, a point emphasized in today's New Testament scholarship. As a faithful Jew, Jesus' practices of eating and drinking were shaped by the covenant tradition as he went forth to proclaim: "The time is fulfilled, and the kingdom of God has come near; repent and believe in the good news" (Mark 1:14-15). In continuity with the messianic promises of the tradition, Jesus Christ's practices are characterized by inclusive communion, the sharing of food with all that are hungry, feasting with joy, and the sacrificial gift of his own body and blood.

Eating in Inclusive Communion. Practices of table-fellowship are important social markers that determine the boundaries of our societies, distinguishing and often dividing people along lines of kinship, class, ethnicity, gender, and political power. The dietary practices of the people of Israel served their vocation to holiness but also created firm divisions between Jews and Gentiles. Varying interpretations of the dietary laws could also generate internal divisions among Jews. The Essenes, a monastic Jewish community, had particularly stringent standards for admission to their communal meals. No women or minors could participate. Even full members of the community were excluded if they were guilty of misconduct or in a state of ritual uncleanness, which could be occasioned by sexual relations or the death of a family member. In this context, Jesus echoes Isaiah's messianic vision of a feast for all people (Isaiah 25:6-7). "Many will come from east and west," he says to the Roman Centurion, a Gentile, "and will eat with Abraham and Isaac and Jacob in the Kingdom of heaven" (Matthew 8:11).

Jesus invites Levi the tax collector to become his disciple and then dines at Levi's home with other guests, and the scribes and the Pharisees question this practice of "eating with sinners and tax collectors" (Mark 2:13-16; cf. Matthew 11:19; Luke 7:34; 19:7). Biblical scholars debate as to whether these "sinners" are Jews whose labor brought them into involuntary contact with impurities, Jews with interpretations of the law that differed from that of the Pharisees, or truly notorious people who acted willfully in abrogation of the Torah. In any case, Jesus replies to his critics: "Those who are well have no need of a physician, but those who are sick; I have come to call not the righteous but sinners" (Mark 2:17).

His table fellowship was an invitation to a restoration of communion, an act of compassionate welcoming that can transform hearts. He invited his followers, in turn, to practices of eating that would heal the divisions of society: "When you give a luncheon or a dinner, do not invite your friends or your brothers or your relatives or rich neighbors, in case they may invite you in return, and you would be repaid. But when you give a banquet, invite the poor, the crippled, the lame, and the blind. And you will be blessed, because they cannot repay you, for you will be repaid at the resurrection of the righteous" (Luke 14:12-14).

Food for All That Hunger. "Ho, everyone who thirsts," extolled Isaiah, "come to the waters; and you that have no money, come, buy, and eat! Come, buy wine and milk without money and without price" (Isaiah 55:1). The prophet's messianic vision is realized on the shore of the Sea of Galilee in a meal shared by a great multitude with neither food nor money. An account of Jesus' act of feeding a large crowd with nothing but a few loaves and fish appears in variant forms in all four Gospels and occurs twice in both Mark and Matthew (Mark 6:32-44; 8:1-10; Matthew 14:13-21; Matthew 15:32-39; Luke 9:10b-17; John 6:1-15). In Mark's first account, Jesus has crossed the Sea of Galilee with his disciples in search of a deserted place to rest. When word goes out that he is nearing the shore, crowds of people arrive from neighboring towns. Jesus "saw a great crowd; and he had compassion for them, because they were like sheep without a shepherd; and he began to teach them many things" (Mark 6:34).

As the hour grew late, the disciples urged Jesus to send the people into the surrounding villages to buy something to eat. "You give them something to eat," Jesus replied

(Mark 6:37). The disciples pointed out that to buy enough bread for a crowd of an estimated five thousand people they would need the wages of two hundred days of labor. "How many loaves do you have?" Jesus responded. They found five loaves and two fish, and Jesus instructed them to arrange the people in groups on the grass.

He blessed the bread and broke the loaves and divided the fish. "And all ate and were filled; and they took up twelve baskets full of broken pieces and of the fish" (Mark 6:42-43). This event echoes the story of the prophet Elisha's feeding of one hundred men with twenty loaves of barley bread (2 Kings 4:42-44) and resonates with accounts of Jesus' prayer of blessing at the Last Supper. Traditionally understood as a miracle story, modern interpretations often explain the feeding of the multitude as an act of communal generosity in which the disciples' initial act of sharing inspires others in the crowd to bring forth bread and fish from their own cloaks and baskets. Whatever happened on the shore of Galilee, comments New Testament scholar John Meier, the multiple attestations of this event in the Gospels is evidence that a very memorable meal took place, a meal with strong eschatological overtones.[45] Jesus spoke of the coming reign of God with the image of a festal banquet in which all who hunger are fed, and on the shore of Galilee that vision became a reality.

Feasting with Joy. "With joy," promised the prophet Isaiah, "you will draw water from the wells of salvation. And you will say in that day: Give thanks to the LORD, call on his name; make known his deeds among the nations; proclaim that his name is exalted" (Isaiah 12:3). Jesus' practices of eating and drinking and many of his parables are characterized by the joy of a wedding feast or a great banquet. In the Gospel of John, the first sign that Jesus performs takes place in the context of a wedding celebration. At Mary's urging, Jesus changes six stone jars of water into wine that is even finer in quality than the wine that has run out (John 2:1-11). The Kingdom of Heaven, Jesus teaches his disciples in Matthew's Gospel, "may be compared to a king who gave a wedding banquet for his son" (Matthew 22:2). Those who were invited did not come, and so the king sent his servants out into the streets to invite everyone to come to the feast. In Luke's moving account of Jesus' parable of the prodigal son, a young man who has squandered his inheritance in dissolute living returns home from a distant country that is ravaged by famine. The son acknowledges his sin to his father, declares his unworthiness to be treated as a son, and asks for the work of a hired hand. "Get the fatted calf and kill it," declared the father, "and let us eat and celebrate; for this son of mine was dead and is alive again; he was lost and is found! And they began to celebrate" (Luke 15:11-24).

Sacrificial Gift of the Body and Blood of Christ. The righteous servant of God, lamented Isaiah, was taken away "by a perversion of justice." The just one was "cut off from the land of the living, stricken for the transgression of my people . . . although he had done no violence, and there was no deceit in his mouth" (Isaiah 53:8-9). Scholars have determined that sometime between the years 28 and 33 c.e., Jesus journeyed to Jerusalem as the feast of Passover approached. According to the Gospel of Mark, he entered the city on the foal of a donkey, in keeping with the prophet Zechariah's messianic vision of the humble king astride a colt who "shall command peace to the nations" (Mark 11:1-11; Zechariah 9:9-10). A furnished guest room had been prepared for Jesus and his apostles to partake of the Passover meal, and when evening came they took their places around the table. In the Gospel of John, Jesus begins the meal by pouring water into a basin and washing all of the apostles' feet (John 13:5), a humble and radical reversal of the culture of the Greco-Roman symposium meal where hosts relished the status that distinguished patrons from guests and masters from servants.

Seated at the table, Jesus Christ took a loaf of bread, blessed it, broke it, and gave it to the apostles. "Take," he said, "this is my body" (Mark 14:22). Then he took a cup of wine, gave thanks, and passed the goblet. "This," he said, "is my blood of the covenant, which is poured out for many. Truly I tell you, I will never again drink of the fruit of the vine until that day when I drink it new in the kingdom of God" (Mark 14:24-25).

After the meal, Jesus and his followers went to an olive orchard just east of Jerusalem, and there Judas betrayed Jesus into the hands of the chief priests, the scribes, and the elders. "Are you the Messiah, the Son of the Blessed One?" the high priest demanded. "I am," said Jesus, and the high priest accused him of blasphemy and determined that he should be condemned to death. The next morning, he handed Jesus over to Pontius Pilate, the Roman Procurator, demanding crucifixion. Pilate had Jesus flogged and then handed him over to his soldiers to be crucified. According to John's account of the Passion, Jesus cried out from the cross, "I am thirsty" (John 19:28). A bystander filled a sponge with sour wine, placed it on a branch of hyssop, and raised it to Jesus' lips, and then he cried loudly and breathed his last.

Joseph of Arimathea received permission from Pilate to take the body of Jesus down from the cross immediately, as it was the day of preparation for the Sabbath. He wrapped the body in a white linen cloth and laid it in a tomb hewn from rock, and he covered the entrance to the tomb with a very large stone. When the Sabbath had passed, Mary Magdalene, Mary the mother of James, and Salome went to the tomb to anoint the body with spices. When they arrived, they found that the stone had been rolled back. "Do not be alarmed," said a young man dressed in a white robe. "You are looking for Jesus of Nazareth, who was crucified. He has been raised; he is not here" (Mark 16:6).

3

the christian practice of eating and drinking

Astonished at the words of the angel, the women went in search of the apostles and recounted all that they had witnessed. The apostles dismissed their words as an idle tale, and Cleopas and his companion left Jerusalem for Emmaus, a village about seven miles away. Walking along dirt roads, they spoke of all that had happened in the preceding days. As they sojourned, they were joined by the risen Christ, whom they did not recognize.

"What are you discussing with each other while you walk along?" he asked.

They recounted with grief all that had transpired in Jerusalem. Jesus interpreted for them the scriptures concerning the Messiah, beginning with Moses and the prophets. Still, they did not know him.

As they approached Emmaus, Cleopas and his companion turned to enter the village, while Jesus continued walking. "Stay with us," they urged, "because it is almost evening and the day is now nearly over."

So Jesus accompanied them, and while they were at table, he took bread in his hands. He blessed the bread, broke it, and shared it among them. Their eyes opened in recognition—and then Christ vanished from their sight.

*Immediately, they returned to Jerusalem in search of the
others and told them what had transpired on the road to
Emmaus, and how the risen Christ had been made known
to them in the breaking of the bread (Luke 24:13-35).*

Two thousand years have hence passed. If Cleopas and
his companion were sojourning through our land today,
would they recognize Christ in our breaking of the bread?
Would they know Christ in my morning coffee of uncertain
origin, my breakfast cereal derived in part from monocultures of corn, my chocolate and bananas, my lonely luncheon value meal, or my dinner of reconstituted chicken
and potatoes?

In the practice of Jesus Christ, eating was an act not
of consumption but communion. In thanksgiving, he
acknowledged that the ultimate source of bread and wine
is the blessing of God. As the incarnation of God's compassion, he fed those who hungered and practiced an inclusive table fellowship that welcomed sinners and outcasts
and transcended the social divisions of his day. A faithful
Jew who came not to abolish but to fulfill the law and the
prophets (Matthew 5:17), he participated in a covenant
tradition that required care for the land and reverence for
the life that God has given to animals. In a consummate
act of communion, he gave his own life for the redemption
of creation and invited his disciples to partake of bread
and wine that is his body and blood.

Christ's resurrection in the power of the Holy Spirit
breaks the bonds of sin and death that originated in our
consumption of the forbidden fruit of Eden. The messianic reign of God's love is both present and not yet fully
accomplished. In the Eucharistic feast, we enjoy a foretaste of the messianic banquet, while in our daily lives we

encounter all too often the reality of a world still in exile from the Paradise of God. Within our world still groaning for the fullness of redemption (Romans 8:22-23), practices of eating and drinking that embody communion are disciplines that conform our lives to Christ and are sacramental signs of the wedding feast to come.

The dominant culture of our society, Wendell Berry observes, assumes that humanity is defined by competition for resources in a market that operates mechanically and measures everything in monetary terms. The assumption of the Bible, in contrast, is that "we are holy creatures living among other holy creatures in a world that is holy." We cannot know that life is holy, however, if we "are content to live with economic practices that daily destroy life and diminish its possibility."[1] Christianity invites us into practices in service of the God who is the source of all holiness and blessing—practices of eating and drinking that mediate our communion with God, the created order, and one another. These practices include fasting, blessing, sharing bread, celebrating the reign of compassion, turning swords into plowshares, feasting, and giving thanks.

Fasting

I am the kind of person who can eat from morning until bedtime, a ceaseless consumer punctuating regular meals with nonstop snacks. Sometimes the snacking comes in response to a genuine growling in my stomach, but sometimes it is simply a palliative or a mindless impulse. Tired of grading papers, overwhelmed by the day's grim news, or reeling from a disagreement with my husband, I gaze into an open refrigerator or rummage through the cupboard.

Is there any chocolate in here anywhere? Perhaps a little piece left over from Christmas? Even just a smidgen?

The practice of eating a little bit here and there more or less constantly throughout the day is known as "grazing," named after the manner in which ruminant animals forage constantly for clover, fescue, or hay. This is a natural practice for sheep and cows at pasture, and perhaps it is also a natural practice for humans, who spent a considerable period of our evolutionary development gathering roots and berries for subsistence. Nonetheless, one of the differences between humans and sheep is that we can make conscious and intentional decisions about food—we can eat, or we can refrain from eating.

Within a tradition that identifies an act of eating as the primal transgression, the act of voluntary abstention from food and drink is a foundational spiritual discipline, and the biblical narratives offer multiple exemplars. Moses ate no bread and drank no water for forty days and forty nights as he stood shrouded in the clouds of Sinai to receive the teachings of the covenant (Exodus 34:28). When he descended from the mountain to find the Israelites reveling before a golden calf, he lay prostrate before the Lord and passed forty days and nights without bread or water (Deuteronomy 9:15-18). When the people of Israel turned to the gods and goddesses of Canaan, Samuel gathered the people in prayer, "and they fasted that day, and said, 'We have sinned against the Lord'" (1 Samuel 7:6). David and his men and all the inhabitants of Jabesh-gilead fasted when they learned that Saul and his three sons had perished in battle with the Philistines (1 Samuel 31:13; 2 Samuel 1:12), and Nehemiah, informed of the lamentable condition of the Jews in Jerusalem who had been spared captivity in Babylon, "sat down and wept, and mourned for days, fasting and praying before the God of heaven" (Nehemiah 1:4). Jesus Christ went forth from the waters of his baptism into the wilderness, where he fasted for forty days and forty nights (Matthew 4:1-4; Luke 4:1-3). "It is written," he said to his tempter, "'One does not live by bread alone, but by every word that comes from the mouth of God.'" (Matthew 4:4; cf. Deuteronomy 8:3)

In the first centuries of the Common Era, Mondays and Wednesdays were Jewish fast days. A strict fast was observed on Yom Kippur, the Day of Atonement, and a lesser fast on dates commemorating historical tragedies such as the destruction of the temple. Christians fasted on Wednesdays and Fridays and for one or more days before Easter. Apostles, prophets, and teachers fasted and prayed before commissioning Barnabas and Saul to go forth and proclaim the word of God (Acts 13:1-3), and Barnabas and Saul in turn fasted when they appointed elders for new churches (Acts 14:23). The *Didache*, a first-century document, is evidence that some Christians fasted for their persecutors and that some churches required fasting of both the baptizer and the catechumen prior to a baptism. In the fourth century, a full forty-day fast was instituted in anticipation of Easter, followed by another forty-day fast before the new observance of celebrating December 25 as the date of Christ's birth. Fasting in these long periods was defined as abstinence from all food until evening—or one meal a day.

Over the course of Christian history, fasting has been practiced in different ways at different times within the diversity of Christian communities. My parents recall that in the Roman Catholicism of their youth, they observed a strict fast from all food and drink from midnight of the evening before their reception of the Eucharist, abstinence from meat on all Fridays of the year, and fasting on all days of Lent except Sunday, defined as taking only one full meal and two smaller meals without meat that together equal less than one full meal. Catholics above the age of fourteen and under the age of sixty also observed fasting and complete abstinence from meat on Ember Days, Ash Wednesday, and on Holy Saturday until noon. The corporate character of these practices made them a defining part of Catholic identity.

It also meant that fasting could become a rote or mechanical observance. In 1966, Pope Paul VI's apostolic constitution *Poenitemini* authorized national bishops' conferences to adapt practices of fasting and abstinence to modern conditions and to allow prayer and charitable works as an alternative means of penitence. The norm for Catholic practice in the United States today is fasting from food and drink for at least one hour before reception of the Eucharist and fasting on Ash Wednesday and Good Friday, defined as taking only one full meal. Abstinence from meat is required on Ash Wednesday and all Fridays during Lent; on every other Friday of the year one may abstain from meat or practice some other penitential discipline.

In a culture in which an estimated 15 percent of women suffer from bulimia or anorexia, illnesses that can be fatal, it is crucial to be very clear about the character of Christian fasting. Fasting is not a matter of counting calories. Nor is it a matter of trying to gain the approval of anyone—least of all God, whose unconditional love for us is manifest in the life, death, and resurrection of Jesus Christ, who welcomed everyone to his table. Fasting is not a matter of punishing the body, nor is it a denial of the goodness of food and the pleasures of eating.

"Why do we and the Pharisees fast often," the disciples of John the Baptist inquired of Jesus, "but your disciples do not fast?"

"The wedding guests," Jesus said to them, "cannot mourn as long as the bridegroom is with them, can they? The days will come when the bridegroom is taken away from them, and then they will fast" (Matthew 9:14-15).

Fasting is an appropriate response to the reality that the Messiah was crucified and that we continue to live in a world that is both redeemed and groaning for the fullness of redemption (Romans 8:22-23). We mourn the ongoing hunger of children, the rape and abuse of women, the persistence of war, the reality of injustice, and the fraying of the ecological webs that sustain life on this planet. We fast, having already tasted the feast of the kingdom—yet still praying. "Your kingdom come" (Matthew 6:10; Luke 11:2).

Fasting is also an act of compassion with all those who are hungry. The uncomfortable experience of a gnawing in my stomach, faintness, and headache is a necessary reminder of the experience of those who cannot voluntarily abstain from food because they simply have nothing to eat. "Hunger" is an abstract problem when I am trying to reorganize the refrigerator to make space for the abundance of spinach, apples, carrots, broccoli, and cider that my husband has brought home from the market. When I myself feel discomforting pangs of contraction in my abdomen, hunger is all too real.

Fasting has served not only as a practice that enables well-fed Christians to empathize with those who have no bread but also as a concrete means of sharing food. "Is not this the fast that I choose: to loose the bonds of injustice, to undo the thongs of the yoke, to let the oppressed go free, and to break every yoke? Is it not to share your bread with the hungry, and bring the homeless poor into your house?" (Isaiah 58:6-7) These words of the prophet Isaiah are proclaimed each year in the Jewish liturgy of the fast of Yom Kippur and the Catholic liturgy of Ash Wednesday. Fasting without almsgiving, preached John Chrysostom (ca. 329–407 c.e.), is not truly fasting at all. According to the *Didache*, Christian households anticipating visits from apostles fasted for days in order to reserve enough food both to serve their guests and give alms. "When someone is poor among them who has need of help," Aristides wrote to Emperor Hadrian about the Christians he had observed, "they fast for two or three days, and they have the custom of sending him the food which they had prepared for themselves."[2] Fasting and almsgiving, Augustine preached, are together the two wings of prayer.

Noting the self-discipline with which athletes prepare themselves to compete for a perishable wreath, Paul enjoined the community at Corinth to train themselves for an imperishable prize (1 Corinthians 9:24-27). Fasting is a discipline that can train our bodies and souls in the ways of compassion, just as the rigorous disciplines of swimmers and gymnasts form them into athletes accomplished in their chosen sport. Christian fasting is not a repression of desire for food and drink, but an opportunity to temporarily distance ourselves from both the biological instinct to eat whatever desirable nut or berry is within reach and the cultural conditioning to "Feed Your Craving," a message that flashed across the digital screen at the register of a fast-food restaurant I once patronized. In this transcendence of our conditioning, we may grow in the virtue of temperance and return to the practice of eating with a pleasure deepened by the integration of the freedom of the human will and the gift of the Holy Spirit.

Fasting, Thomas Ryan writes in *Fasting Rediscovered*, also reminds us that we are creatures utterly dependent on the fruits of God's creation for a sustenance we do not take for granted when we abstain from food. As we break through our conditioned reflex of self-gratification, we may also discover that we are creatures whose desire is not simply for food and drink but also for God. Arlene Becker describes the ultimate purpose and fruit of fasting as a union with divine love. In fasting, she told Ryan, "I've discovered my prayers for others carry more love—and the power of love heals, blesses, and brings life."[3]

Although sometimes associated with dualistic spiritualities, fasting can bring life and healing to the body as well as the soul. We are embodied spirits, Ryan emphasizes, and the discipline that cultivates virtue in our souls may also strengthen and cleanse our bodies. The process of chewing, digesting, and assimilating food takes a tremendous degree of energy, and fasting even for short periods gives our bodies a beneficial rest. When the body abstains from food for an extended period of time, it begins to break down tissues to provide the energy and proteins we need to survive. In its wisdom, it feeds first on reserves of fat that harbor accumulated toxins and on tissues that are damaged and diseased.

Fasting is a practice that anyone other than a growing child, pregnant woman, nursing mother, elder, or a person with a metabolic disorder or some other infirmity can undertake in a time and place best suited to the rhythm of the person's own life. It is also a spiritual discipline much enhanced by a corporate practice. "The greatest religious phenomenon in the world today," Charles Murphy reflects in *The Spirituality of Fasting: Rediscovering a Christian Practice*, "is Ramadan, during which millions of

[Muslims] all over the world, together, publically fast and pray."[4] Eamon Duffy laments that the change in norms for fasting and abstinence in Roman Catholicism replaced a weekly observance with "a genteel and totally individualistic injunction to do some penitential act on a Friday—an injunction, incidentally, that most Catholics know nothing about."[5] Orthodox Christians practice together an ecclesial fast from all foods derived from animals for 180 days of the liturgical year. "In our church," comments Deborah Kostoff, a member of Christ Our Savior Holy Spirit Orthodox Church in Norwood, Ohio, "we look forward to the Lenten fast. We need that time of focus and discipline. And the liturgies are so beautiful." On Clean Monday, the first day of Great Lent, the Orthodox sing, "With joy let us enter upon the beginning of the Fast. Let us not be of sad countenance."

Blessing

I was tired after the trip from Cincinnati to Cambridge, and I imagined that someone who had traveled all the way from Poland would be even more fatigued. Those of us who had gathered to participate in an event of inter-religious dialogue had just finished breakfast, and sitting across from me at a table of dark solid oak was a Jewish professor from Warsaw. Having completed his morning meal, he bowed his head and closed his eyes.

"Jet lag?" I asked.

He held out an upright hand with open palm in a silent gesture I recognized to mean "wait."

Moments later, he raised his head and explained simply, "The prayer after eating bread."

In my scramble to get everyone out of the door in time for school and work, I often neglect to pray before the morning meal, and I have never once prayed afterward. I do not typically eat bread for breakfast, but I was nonetheless humbled by the practice of my Jewish colleague.

The Gospels give us an indication of Jesus Christ's own practice of prayer before meals. When his disciples produced five loaves and two fish with which to feed the crowds who had followed them to a deserted place, Jesus "looked up to heaven, and blessed and broke the loaves" (Mark 6:41; Luke 9:10-17; John 6:10-13; cf. Mark 8:1-10). Gathered with his apostles to share the Passover meal before his crucifixion, he "took a loaf of bread, and when he had given thanks, he broke it and gave it to them" (Luke 22:19). These words of benediction and thanksgiving spoken before a meal are prayers of blessing.

Prayers of blessing increased in importance after Rome destroyed the temple in Jerusalem in 70 C.E. With the abrupt end of the temple sacrifices, the rabbis taught the people to make temples of their homes and hearts and to offer a perpetual sacrifice of praise. In the Mishnah, a compendium of Jewish teachings from the period 200 B.C.E. through 200 C.E., the first section of the division *Zeraim* (Seeds), which discusses agricultural practices, is the tractate *Berachot* (Benedictions). Today, an observant Jew prays words of blessing upon rising in the morning, upon washing, upon eating, upon finishing a meal, and on multiple other occasions. The rabbis taught that one should offer no less than 100 blessings over the course of a day. Blessings over meals include a prayer said before eating foods such as lentils or lettuce grown in the soil: "Blessed are You, Adonai our God, Ruler of the Universe, who creates the fruit of the earth." Before eating apples or pears or figs, one prays, "Blessed are You, Adonai our God, Ruler of the Universe, who creates the fruit of the tree." Over bread and wine, one prays: "Blessed are You, Adonai our God, Ruler of the Universe, who brings forth bread from the earth" and "creates the fruit of the vine." Before eating or drinking any other food or beverage, one prays, "Blessed are You, Adonai our God, Ruler of the Universe, through Whose word everything came to be."[6]

In the classification systems of ecological science, a creature can be either a "producer" who makes food directly from the energy of the sun, a "decomposer" who breaks down dead organisms so they can become food for others, or a "consumer." According to the Jewish mystical tradition, however, there is more to reality than that which meets the strictly scientific eye. Human beings are not only consumers, but also creatures with a unique role to play in the mediation of the healing of our fractured world. If we do nothing but thoughtlessly consume, Rabbi Marcia Prager explains in *The Path of Blessing*, we readily become despoilers. But if we live with an expanded consciousness of awe and wonder and return to God the love that flows throughout the entire cosmos, we walk in the path of blessing.

> "Blessed are You, Adonai our God, Ruler of the Universe, who brings forth bread from the earth" and "creates the fruit of the vine."

Blessing, writes biblical scholar Claus Westermann in *Blessing in the Bible and the Life of the Church*, is one of two fundamental modes of God's presence. Scripture distinguishes God's saving acts of deliverance (such as the exodus from slavery and the resurrection of Jesus Christ) and God's life-giving power of wisdom that upholds, sustains, and undergirds the created order. This is the power of blessing. It is the power of the great diversity of life: God blessed the birds that fly above the earth and every living creature with which the waters swarm and God said, "Be fruitful and multiply" (Genesis 1:22). It is the power of human generation and the fecundity of the land: "If you heed these ordinances . . . , the LORD your God will maintain with you the covenant loyalty that he swore to your ancestors; he will love you, bless you, and multiply you; he will bless the fruit of your womb and the fruit of your ground, your grain and your wine and your oil, the increase of your cattle and the issue of your flock" (Deuteronomy 7:12-13). Blessing is *shalom*—peace, well-being, harmony, and wholeness: "The LORD bless you and keep you; the LORD make his face to shine upon you, and be gracious to you; the LORD lift up his countenance upon you, and give you peace" (Numbers 6:24-26).

Words of blessing said over a meal are a celebration of the teeming life of birds and sea creatures, the fecundity and diversity of plants and trees, the fertility of land watered by gentle rain, and the health and well-being of children. "Bless us, O Lord, and these thy gifts, which we are about to receive, from your bounty, through Christ our Lord." Can I pray with integrity these words of Christian blessing over all the meals that I have eaten? Can I ask God to bless a cup of morning coffee brewed from beans that may have been harvested by hungry children? Or a luncheon hamburger of unknown origin that may exist only because land that was once the magnificent Amazon rainforest teeming with life was cleared for cattle fodder? "How are we to say grace," laments L. Shannon Jung, "over food disorders?"[7]

When I receive the gift of good food that has been cultivated with care for God's creation, awe and gratitude rise spontaneously. Last summer, most of our produce came from Earth Shares, a community-supported agriculture (CSA) program on land stewarded by the Grail community in Loveland, Ohio. The early spring lettuce was vibrant with deep green color and crisper and sweeter than any lettuce I can remember ever having tasted. Weeks later, it was the basis for salads that included tangy red radishes, heirloom tomatoes, and aromatic sweet basil. Out of the dark earth came onions white as snow and lumpy potatoes so inherently flavorful I could make soup with no seasoning other than a pinch of salt. As I write, it is now winter, and we are still relishing the hearty butternut squash that stores well in cool weather until it comes steaming orange out of the oven.

Mary Lu Lageman and Steve Edwards, head gardeners of the CSA, grow thirty-five different kinds of heirloom and hybrid vegetables using sustainable organic methods. "We treat the soil with respect," Mary Lu explains, "for it is a living entity comprised of inorganic and organic life forms. We feed the soil with horse manure and composted leaves from the city of Loveland. This compost is also a living entity rich in microorganisms that decompose the organic matter in a manner that enables it to be used by plants." To minimize damage to the soil, the tilling and clearing of weeds is done with a small tractor, a non-mechanized wheel hoe, or the human hand. Healthy soil generates healthy plants that have the resilience to withstand pests and disease. Strips of companion plants are sown between the rows of vegetables to attract beneficial insects like ladybugs, and if a pest problem does emerge, it is diagnosed and addressed with measures such as crop

rotations, crop successions, or the introduction of a species (like wasp) that feeds on an unwelcome insect (like
aphids). Throughout the terrible drought we endured last
July and August, the gardens were watered primarily with
chlorine-free rainwater collected in a pond during the
spring. Members of the CSA contributed to the labor necessary for the harvest and witnessed the mysterious trans-
formation of seed, water, and soil into kale, green beans,
and carrots. With hands immersed in dark moist soil, I
spontaneously join in the joyful prayer of the psalmist:

> Bless the LORD, O my soul.
>   O LORD, my God, you are very great. . . .
> You cause the grass to grow for the cattle,
>   and plants for people to use,
>   you bring forth food from the earth
>   (Psalm 104:1, 14).

Some churches in my region have organized CSAs or
established farmers' markets in church parking lots that
build networks of mutual support between urban dwellers
and farmers. Other churches participate in fair trade organizations that build relationships of equity between the people
who grow coffee, cacao, and bananas and the people who
drink and eat these tropical fruits. Members of my parish
regularly sell fair trade coffee and chocolate through Equal
Exchange, an organization that builds long-term relationships with small farming cooperatives in places like Peru,
Nicaragua, and the Dominican Republic. Some of the cooperatives grow cacao under a shade canopy of mixed trees
that provides habitat for migrating songbirds in the winter,
and all of them use organic growing methods. I spoke with a
representative of Equal Exchange to inquire about the living

conditions of the families that are part of the cooperatives, and she told me that it varies considerably. She has traveled to several of these places and lived with some of the families, so she speaks with firsthand experience. Historic inequities continue to shape the relationships between people in North America and the peoples of Central America and the Caribbean, but these fair trade relationships have been for many people a path of blessing.

Sharing Bread

Many people in my city of Cincinnati have no easy access to fair trade coffee or even locally grown apples or potatoes. Like many other major metropolitan areas, Cincinnati has several "urban food deserts," neighborhoods void of farm stands or supermarkets. Residents shop in corner stores with shelves decked primarily in glossy packages of chips and brightly colored cans of carbonated sodas. Residents of these neighborhoods may eat and drink but still be malnourished.

All across the United States, the shadow of hunger has grown deeper since the advent of the recession in December 2007. According to the Food Research and Action Center's analysis of data from the Gallup-Healthways Well-Being Index, in nearly every state of the union at least one person in seven did not have enough money to buy food for themselves or their family at some point during 2010. Forty-seven states and the District of Columbia had food hardship rates of 14.5 percent or higher. Seventeen percent of Americans— or 50 million people—now live in households classified by the U.S. Department of Agriculture as "food insecure."[8]

In the parable of the sheep and the goats, the Son of Man seated upon the throne of glory states that one who gives food and drink to the least of the members of his family does so also for him and will inherit the kingdom (Matthew 25:31-46). Today the "least of these" include approximately one-third of the human family. The United Nations' 2010 Human Development Report, based on data from 104 countries, states that despite gains in some areas, one-third of the people in these countries (1.75 billion people) live with acute deprivations. Across the globe, economic recession, rising oil prices, the demand for grain for use as animal fodder and biofuels, and climate instability are deepening the pain of human hunger. "We are facing one crisis after another," explains Sheila Sisulu, executive director for hunger solutions of the United Nations World Food Program, adding that the effects "are disproportionately affecting the poorest and most vulnerable—those who are least responsible for the crises."[9] Catholic Relief Services corroborates the UN reports with personal accounts of people like Efrain and his family in Sabinal, Guatemala, who lost their entire crop of maize, beans, wheat, and potatoes when rivers flooded after eight days of storms. In Ethiopia, Teshome's efforts to grow carrots for his children have been plagued by drought.[10]

Prolonged hunger, as distinct from protracted voluntary fasting, is physically and spiritually harmful to adults and will permanently scar a child. "We have an absolutely crucial window of opportunity during pregnancy and the first 24 months of a child's life to prevent stunting," Sisulu emphasizes. "Stunted at two years of age means stunted for life, with long-term consequences in terms of health, education, and productivity."[11]

Standing in my kitchen, which is fully stocked with gallon jars of a diverse array of colorful beans and cupboards full of rice and pasta, I have a hard time truly grasping the scale of hunger in the world or really knowing what it is like to be a mother who cannot feed her children. It is hard to fathom the suffering behind the statistic that 17,000 children die of hunger each day.[12]

In *Hunger: An Unnatural History*, Sharman Russell recalls leafing through a newspaper in a booth at a fast-food restaurant where she was dining with her five-year-old son. A story of a famine that featured a photo of a child caught her eye. "The fat in her tissues had been used up long ago, so that her skin looked loose and her eyes sunk into bone. Her brain needed glucose of which the only source now was her own protein. . . . Soon she would eat the muscles in her arms, in her legs, in her heart." Russell's son, meanwhile, needed help assembling the cardboard toy nestled between the warm french fries and burger. "I wanted to snatch this little girl from the page," she recalls. And then "I pushed hard against the gate [of grief]. . . . *This was not my baby.* I did not burst out crying."[13]

In a world in which some are well fed while others die of starvation, I am the rich man dressed in fine clothes who dines sumptuously every day (Luke 16:19-31). I see no Lazarus covered in sores looking for crumbs outside my window. That, however, is only because it is my privilege to live in a place where I am shielded from views of his need. Like Sharman, I push hard against the gate. "We are afraid," she reflects, "that the pain of other people will subtract the joy from our life, that our joy will be impossible next to their pain." A child dying of hunger "shatters the view from the kitchen window."[14]

"Bless, Lord, this meal from which we draw the strength to serve you. Give bread to those who have none, and hunger and thirst for justice to those who have plenty." This is the daily prayer before meals at the Community of the Ark in the mountains of south central France, a community founded by Lanza del Vasto, a Christian who studied with Gandhi. The Christian tradition includes multiple practices like this prayer that may help open the gate of my heart to those in need.

On Ash Wednesday, Catholic families take home from church a cardboard bowl in which to collect money saved from foods not eaten in times of fast and abstinence. Catholic Relief Services uses the funds collected in this Operation Rice Bowl to provide immediate assistance to the hungry and to help people around the world grow crops, access clean water, build schools, and start small businesses.

Hunger knows no season, and something comparable can be practiced all year round. In a homily on Acts, John Chrysostom (ca. 349–407) recalled the story of the hospitality of Sarah and Abraham and urged members of his church to set aside a room in their homes for Christ: "Say, 'This is Christ's room; this is set apart for him.' Even if it is very simple, he will not disdain it. Christ goes about 'naked and a stranger'; he needs shelter: do not hesitate to give it to him."[15] And so I set an extra place at our table, and my son decorates a cardboard box with photos of children from all around the world, clipped with angular lines from mission magazines. Into the box he will put a portion of the money we spend on the evening meal. It can go to Catholic Relief Services, the Catholic Campaign for Human Development, or the Land Institute—organizations that are feeding people, empowering people to feed themselves, and caring for the land that feeds us all.

Sharing bread can be done both in our homes and in our ecclesial communities. Once a month, some members of my parish prepare and serve a meal for sixty people at

Tender Mercies, an organization that provides housing and services to people with special mental and emotional needs. Some support Grace Place, a Catholic Worker House of Hospitality. Others are members of the Saint Vincent de Paul Society and make home visits every Saturday to persons in the neighborhoods surrounding Bellarmine Chapel. They return with stories of homes with multiple children, empty cupboards, and beds that are nothing more than coats layered on hard floors.

A striking example of a corporate practice of the sharing of bread is that of St. Gregory's Episcopal Church in San Francisco, California. One Sunday, newcomer Sara Miles received communion for the first time and burst into tears at her recognition that the bread she had partaken was truly the body of Christ. A former journalist who had received sustenance from impoverished people while living in war zones in Central America, she was struck by the words engraved with gilt letters on the polished hardwood altar: "This fellow welcomes sinners and eats with them" (Luke 15:2) and "Did not our Lord share his table with tax collectors and harlots? So do not distinguish between worthy and unworthy. All must be equal for you to love and serve" (Isaac of Nineveh).

Soon after Sara's first communion, a teacher at her daughters' school mentioned that a little boy in the class "talked about food and how he wished they had more of it in his house," and Sara knew immediately what needed to be done: "Feed my sheep" (John 21:17). She learned that there are an estimated ninety thousand hungry people in San Francisco, a city in which someone who works sixty hours a week at a minimum-wage job earns just about enough money to pay rent on a one-bedroom apartment—with no money left over for groceries. She raised funds for regular bulk purchases from a food bank, and once a week she and other volunteers encircled the altar of St. Gregory's with tables piled high with sandwich bread, noodles, potatoes, onions, and fresh oranges and strawberries from California's fertile Central Valley. Sign-in sheets enabled the volunteers to learn the names of their guests and keep track of numbers, but there were no probing questions to answer and no forms to fill out. Jesus, Sara writes in *Take This Bread: A Radical Conversion*, simply welcomes everyone to his table.

Celebrating the Reign of Compassion

As a college student, I was surprised to learn that our capacity to welcome everyone to the table may be constrained by the kinds of foods that we serve. In a philosophy course on food ethics, we read *Food First: Beyond the Myth of Scarcity,* a book by Francis Moore Lappé and Joseph Collins that explained that sixteen pounds of grain are needed to produce just one pound of beef. Land that is growing grain to feed cows could feed many more people if humans ate the grain directly rather than cycling it through cattle or other animals.

Decades since *Food First* was published in 1979, both the world population and the challenges of feeding everyone in the human family have grown. In a world with billions of malnourished people, degraded soils, diminishing sources of water, and a destabilized climate, multiple other voices are calling for a reduction in meat consumption. The average American, writes Paul Roberts in *The End of Food*, eats around nine ounces of meat a day, almost four times the government recommended intake of protein. Calculating the quantity of grain needed to produce a pound of edible feedlot beef (as distinct from one pound of cow), he notes that "it takes a full *twenty* pounds of grain to make a single pound of beef (compared to 4.5 and 7.3 for chicken and pigs, respectively)." Although social assumptions will make our meat-eating habits hard to change, "nearly every credible forecast shows that if we're to have any chance of meeting future food demand in a sustainable fashion, lowering our meat consumption will be absolutely essential."[16]

Diets high in meat and dairy products, echoes Julian Cribb in *The Coming Famine*, use "massively more water than diets based mainly on vegetables and grains"; they also increase our dependency on artificial fertilizers and use three times more energy than vegetarian diets.[17] Our meat consumption is also a major contributing factor to climate change, which is adversely affecting global food production. *Livestock's Long Shadow*, a 2006 report of the United Nations Food and Agriculture Organization, found livestock production responsible for 18 percent of all global greenhouse gas emissions, including carbon dioxide, methane, and nitrous oxide.[18] "Please eat less meat," urged Dr. Rajendra Pachauri, in his capacity as chair of the UN's Intergovernmental Panel on Climate Change (IPCC), "in terms of immediacy of action and the feasibility of bringing about reductions in a short period of time, it clearly is the most attractive opportunity."[19]

Voices like these confirmed what I had learned years ago in my college food ethics course: in a world of (now) 6.9 billion people, eating lower on the food chain is a necessary practice if we are to ameliorate the hunger of the human family. What I had not considered in the ethics course was the life and death of the animal that is also at stake in our decisions about food and agriculture. Both the

Noahide and Mosaic covenants require reverence for the life that God gives to animals. In the Orthodox Church, one of the multiple reasons for fasting from meat, dairy products, and eggs for long portions of the liturgical year is the Christic restoration of the peaceable conditions of Eden, where humans lived in harmony with the animals and ate a diet of grains, nuts, plants, and fruit. Saint Isaac the Syrian, a seventh-century bishop and theologian, writes of the compassionate heart that is "burning with love for the whole creation, for humans, for the birds, for the beasts . . . for all creatures." This heart "can no longer bear to see or learn from others of any suffering, even the smallest pain being inflicted upon any creature."[20]

In the United States today, 99 percent of broiler chickens, 90 percent of pigs, and most cattle and dairy cows spend all or most of their lives in what have been dubbed "factory farms," livestock production centers that operate with a machine-like efficiency. Like the caged chickens that were the most likely source of the nuggets in my convenient frozen dinner, cows and pigs are crowded into tightly confined spaces and denied the opportunity to act on their natural desires—a sow's desire to root in the ground for food, build a nest, and suckle her young, or a cow's need to graze in pasture or rest beneath the shade of a tree. "Animals, too, are God's creatures. . . ." Cardinal Joseph Ratzinger (now Pope Benedict XVI) commented in a 2002 interview. "Certainly, a sort of industrial use of creatures, so that geese are fed in such a way as to produce as large a liver as possible, or hens live so packed together that they become just caricatures of birds, this degrading of living creatures to a commodity seems to me in fact to contradict the relationship of mutuality that comes across in the Bible."[21]

Over the course of the past decades, studies have shown that mother cows have deep emotional bonds with their young and that pigs have genuine intelligence. Ethical reflection on the character of our relationship with animals has become an important discipline within the field of philosophy and is beginning to receive attention in theology through the work of scholars such as Andrew Linzey, director of the Oxford Centre for Animal Ethics. In *The School of Compassion: A Roman Catholic Theology of Animals*, Deborah M. Jones articulates a Catholic ethic of life that maintains a moral distinction between humans and animals but also calls upon us to live in such a way as to avoid or minimize animals' pain and suffering. Given that even on the best of farms, animals end their lives in a slaughterhouse, this principle leads her to an ethic of Christian abstinence from meat in all circumstances when other sources of food are available.

In the Christian theologies of Linzey and Jones, the vegetarianism I had embraced as a youth in my college food ethics course received yet more confirmation. And then I read Michael Pollan, a man who espouses the basic rule "Eat food. Not too much. Mostly plants." Even so, chapter 17 of Pollan's book *The Omnivore's Dilemma* opens with "The Steakhouse Dialogues," an imaginary conversation with Peter Singer held in a restaurant over a medium-rare rib-eye steak. Pollan acknowledges the compelling character of many of the arguments of his imaginary conversation partner, the world's leading philosopher of animal rights. The exclusion of the pain of animals from our moral consideration, Pollan concludes, may indeed implicate us in "speciesism," and the growing interest in the practice of vegetarianism may be a sign that human civilization is "groping toward a higher plane of consciousness."[22] At the same time, Pollan notes the signs of true animal happiness he has observed on farms where pigs and cows and chickens are treated well, and he wonders if a vision of a vegan utopia is a reflection of an urban culture out of touch with the way nature really works.

On Polyface Farm in northern Virginia, Pollan witnessed Joel Salatin orchestrating a farm that emulates the natural symbiosis of plants, soil, animals, and birds. Salatin keeps cattle moving across multiple pastures so they don't chew the grass in any one spot so low as to eat the blaze of growth from which the plant can regenerate. Meanwhile, the grass, having lost its blade, balances itself by shedding root hairs, a process that builds humus and regenerates soil. As the cows forage around the pasture for tasty bites of fescue or clover, they drop manure that further fertilizes the earth. Once they have moved on to new ground, Salatin brings in the laying hens, who flock across fields shorn to a navigable height in search of tasty bugs lurking in the clumps of manure. This removes potential parasites from the fields, and the chickens also serve the farm by leaving behind their own nitrogen-rich droppings. Back at their roost, they lay eggs with deep yellow yolks that are the pride of Charlotteville's best chefs. Mark Bittman, who has documented the unsustainable character of our meat consumption, notes that it takes 2.2 calories of fossil fuel energy to produce one calorie of corn but a full 40 calories of fossil fuel to produce a single calorie of beef protein.[23] This equation, however, presumes a system in which feedlot cattle eat grain grown with fossil fuels that their bodies are not designed to digest. At Polyface, the cows eat grass grown with the energy of the sun—a plant their rumens are uniquely adapted to convert into a usable food source in a way that our human stomachs are not.

Are farms like Salatin's carefully orchestrated pasture a keystone part of the solar-powered farming of our future? No, argue those who point out that the fermentation process by which the bacteria in bovine rumens turns grass into assimilable nourishment produces large quantities of methane, a global warming gas twenty-three times more potent than carbon dioxide. Yes, insist those who emphasize that a pasturing process like that of Salatin builds humus rather than eroding topsoil, removing carbon from the atmosphere and sequestering it in the ground.

Whether farms like Polyface are a bane or boon in our world of shrinking glaciers and wild weather, the fact remains that Salatin's chickens end their lives under the blade of a knife. He slaughters them himself in the open air with every effort to minimize their pain. Killing animals, nonetheless, is inescapably a bloody act. Thinking of St. Isaac's compassionate heart, I try to imagine a farm like Polyface that would pasture only dairy cows and raise chickens solely for eggs. Probe further, says my husband the ethicist, and you will find that in order to be economically viable, farms that raise dairy cows have to separate the male calves from their mothers and sell them to be raised for veal, and farms that breed laying hens have to kill all the male chicks.

The Genesis account of eating in Eden was a vision of a lost garden, not a description of reality. Today, anthropologists and evolutionary biologists attempting to interpret an incomplete fossil record conclude that hominid diets were primarily plant-based but that high-quality meat was a rewarding supplement whose importance increased in significance during the evolution of the *Homo* clade. And what of us today? Are we so far east of Eden that we cannot develop an agricultural system that is simultaneously capable of feeding everyone, compassionate in its relation to animals, and ecologically sustainable in the coming post-petroleum world? Is it possible to produce our food in a manner that is a sign of the messianic kingdom promised by the prophet Isaiah, the reign of *shalom* when "the wolf shall live with the lamb, and the leopard shall lie down with the kid" (Isaiah 11:6-9; cf. 65:25)? "If the carnivorous animal will disappear at the end of time," comments Samuel Dresner in *The Jewish Dietary Laws*, "how much more so the carnivorous man?"[24]

According to some Jewish interpretations of Scripture, the dietary practices outlined in Leviticus are a preparation for the peaceable kingdom that Isaiah envisioned. The laws distinguishing pure and impure animals prevent humans from eating animals that are themselves carnivorous. This protects the people of Israel from eating the flesh of animals that have eaten the blood of other animals and also mitigates the transference of animal instincts and passions to humans. The body, writes Samson Raphael Hirsch, is an instrument of the spirit, and vegetable foods, or the flesh of herbivorous animals, are more appropriate for human consumption than the flesh of carnivorous beasts, which may make us indifferent to loftier, moral impulses.[25] Rabbi Abraham Isaac Kook interprets the restrictions on animal consumption in Leviticus as pedagogical measures cultivating a reverence for life that will ultimately lead Israel away from all flesh consumption.[26] In the messianic era, there will be no animal sacrifices in the restored Temple in Jerusalem—only an offering of grain.

Christians profess that the messianic era has begun in the life, death, and resurrection of Jesus Christ. An important sign of the advent of this era was the table fellowship between Jews and Gentiles that occurred in Peter's visit to the home of the Roman centurion Cornelius and in the churches founded by Paul. Peter's visit was preceded by a vision of a sheet bearing animals that was lowered from heaven as a voice declared, "What God has made clean, you must not call profane" (Acts 10:1-48), and Paul assured communities in Galatia and Rome that the resurrection of Christ and the gift of the Holy Spirit frees Gentile converts from obligation to Mosaic observances (Galatians 2:15—4:7; Romans 2:1—8:39). These accounts in Acts and Paul, coupled with Jesus' statement that "there is nothing outside a person that by going in can defile, but the things that come out are what defile" (Mark 7:15), have led many Christians to conclude that Jesus relaxed the dietary law and abrogated the distinction between clean and unclean animals. Yet, notes New Testament scholar John Meier, differences in the eating practices of Jews and Gentiles were a major source of debate among the first generation of Christians, and "neither Paul nor the disputing parties in Luke's narrative ever think of appealing to the teaching of Jesus on the subject, be it the logion of Mark 7:15 or some other saying."[27] Peter has a revelatory vision that enables him to embrace Cornelius; Paul appeals to the resurrection; and at the Council of Jerusalem, the matter of Gentile nonobservance of Jewish dietary practices is resolved with a pragmatic compromise and an eschatological interpretation of Amos 9:11-12 (Acts 15:13-29). Mark, writing somewhere around the year 70 c.e., says Jesus "declared all foods clean" (Mark 7:19), but Meier doubts that this text originated with the historical Jesus. It is far more likely that the new situation generated by the death and resurrection of Jesus Christ led to new practices and that these new practices influenced the composition of Mark's Gospel.

Today we are again in a new situation, and perhaps there is need once more to reconstruct some of our practices of eating and drinking. We need dietary practices befitting the inauguration of Christ's reign of compassion—practices like abstinence from meat, milk, cheese, or eggs produced in conditions that violate the well-being of animals. The question as to whether or not it is ethical for twenty-first-century Christians to eat meat or other animal products at all is a very complicated matter, and people of goodwill have come to a range of conclusions. One ecclesial practice appropriate to our profession of faith in Christ would be abstinence from meat on Sunday, the feast of the resurrection that marks the inbreaking of the messianic age. This observance would not be an act of penitence, but rather a celebration of the restoration of the Edenic harmony of all creatures promised by the prophet Isaiah (Isaiah 11:6-9). In the resurrection, reflects Saint Ephrem the Syrian, God will renew both earth and heaven, "liberating all creatures, granting them paschal joy, along with us."[28]

Turning Swords into Plowshares

I had long thought that Isaiah's messianic language about "beating swords into plowshares" (Isaiah 2:4; cf. Micah 4:3) was a prophetic metaphor—a powerful one, but a metaphor nonetheless. Then I read in a journal of biblical studies that turning swords into plowshares is precisely what people in ancient Israel did in times of peace. The mineral ores available to them were limited, and the metals they mined had to serve multiple purposes. Our own culture has been slow to recognize that minerals—and topsoil, water, potassium, and nitrogen—are all limited goods. A decision to use the goods of the earth in one manner means they will not be available for other ends.

For decades, most Americans and others in affluent sectors of the global population have enjoyed a profusion and abundance of inexpensive food unimaginable in prior eras of human history. In the latter part of the twentieth century, the global food system produced more than enough calories for everyone; people went hungry not for lack of global production, but for lack of equitable patterns of land ownership and equitable systems of sharing the fruits of the earth. This cornucopia of plenty, however, was generated through practices that are unsustainable, and we are now entering a period of scarcity. Between 2001 and 2008, human beings and our livestock consumed more grain than we produced, and the UN's Food and Agriculture Organization (FAO) reports that food prices rose an average of 80 percent between 2005 and 2008. "The world," Cribb emphasizes in *The Coming Famine*, "has ignored the ominous constellation of factors that now make feeding humanity sustainably our most pressing task."[29]

This constellation of factors includes a dramatic decline in the diversity of our agricultural seed, as countryside tapestries of profuse varieties of cultivars have given way to vast monocultures of corn and soy that are just as vulnerable to disease as monocultures of Gros Michel bananas. In the United States, there has been an exodus from the land of farmers who could not compete with agribusiness, a loss of the intergenerational transfer of agricultural wisdom from parents to children, and a decimation of rural communities. Farmland is being sold for commercial and retail development at the rate of 2,880 acres a day. On land exposed by the plow to wind and rain, soil erosion proceeds at a rate of one inch every twenty-five years, which far exceeds the rate of natural soil formation. On most farms, the fertility of the remaining soil is sustained only by the application of nitrogen, phosphorous, and potassium fertilizers—manufactured (in the case of nitrogen) from natural gas, an element projected to become increasingly scare, or mined (in the case of potassium) from potash, which is also in limited supply. Between 1945 and 1989, crop losses from insect damage in the United States nearly doubled from 7 percent to 13 percent, despite a nearly tenfold increase in the quantity of chemical pesticides applied. Today, nearly 325 active pesticide compounds are legally permitted for use in the production of 675 basic forms of food, and residues can be found on our dinner tables, in the umbilical cords of newborn infants, and in samples taken from our children's urine.[30] Irrigation is necessary to the cultivation of nearly half of our food, and sources of water are diminishing; the huge Ogallala Aquifer, for example, which tunnels under the border of eight western states, is being depleted at a pace ten times faster than the rate of natural recharge. And with climate change now under way, we face rising average global temperatures and an increase in the intensity and frequency of floods, droughts, and other extreme weather events; in the summer of 2010, record heat shrank Russia's grain harvest from approximately 100 million to 60 million tons. To mitigate the effects of climate change, scientists have called for dramatic reductions in our combustion of fossil fuels, but that will be difficult to do when our agricultural system is heavily dependent on oil to power large machinery, produce petrochemicals, and transport food over long distances. In a sense, writes Dale Allen Pfeiffer, we are now "eating fossil fuels."[31] This will have to change; Dr. Faith Birol, chief economist of the International Energy Agency, estimates that sometime between 2010 and 2020, global production of oil will peak and then begin an irreversible decline, even as the industrialization of India and China continues to accelerate demand.

In our own households and churches, we can observe practices of eating and drinking that share bread with those who are hungry and support farmers who steward God's earth. Even the best of these practices, however, will not be sufficient in scale or scope to prevent the deepening of the global food crisis. Like Joseph, who warned Pharaoh of a coming famine, churches can be a public voice calling attention to the skeletal cows that are again rising from the banks of the Nile. Christians can bring the best of our moral and spiritual traditions into conversation with the best of ecological and agricultural science and engage the public in discussion about the local, national, and international policies that will be necessary to ensure the provision of daily bread for all into the future.

Cribb emphasizes that food shortages will precipitate conflict and violence in a world still armed with nuclear weapons, and he describes action to ensure the global food supply as "an essential form of defense." He calls for a transfer of a portion of the $1.5 trillion the world spends annually on armaments to budgets for food security; at the turn of the millennium, the combined public investment of all governments in food production was just $23 billion—"as if killing one another were fifty times more important to us than eating."[32] Problems, he explains, are not solved by money alone, but there is an urgent need for investment in the research and development of conservation agriculture and ecological methods of farming. In *The End of Food*, Paul Roberts also calls for immediate public investment in sustainable regional food systems.

In October 2008, Michael Pollan published an open letter in the *New York Times Magazine* to whomever would be elected that November as the nation's next "Farmer-in-Chief." He stressed that the reform of our entire food system should be the new president's highest priority, and he offered a vision of a national network of decentralized, resilient, solar-powered farms stewarded by a new generation of young farmers who use diverse polycultures, pastured animals, and perennialized grains to build soil, sequester carbon, and support the health and well-being of ecosystems and human persons. In January 2009, Wendell Berry and Wes Jackson, farmers who have for decades practiced precisely this kind of farming, asked our nation's leaders to move beyond the shortsightedness of our typical agricultural legislation and develop a Fifty-Year Farm Bill that can lead us into a viable future. The visions of Berry, Jackson, and Pollan embody many of the principles set forth by Catholic social teaching to guide action in the public realm: respect for the dignity of the human person created in the image of God, service of the common good, special attention to the needs of the poor and vulnerable, preservation of the integrity of creation and stewardship of God's earth, support for local and regional economic and civic structures that connect us to the land and build strong communities, and solidarity with all peoples and creatures.

Feasting

> On this mountain, the Lord of hosts will make for all peoples
>   a feast of rich food, a feast of well-aged wines,

of rich food filled with marrow, of well-aged wines
strained clear.
And he will destroy on this mountain
the shroud that is cast over all peoples,
the sheet that is spread over all nations;
he will swallow up death forever.
Then the Lord God will wipe away the tears from all
faces,
and the disgrace of his people he will take away
from all the earth,
for the Lord has spoken.

Isaiah 25:6-8

In both Jewish and Christian literature, visions of the
messianic era feature the celebration of an eschatological banquet. In Christianity, the Eucharist is a foretaste
of the kingdom in which people will come from east and
west to eat with Abraham and Isaac and Jacob (Matthew
8:11). The Eucharistic banquet is a feast to which everyone is invited, a meal where all who hunger and thirst
may come and drink wine without price and eat the bread
that truly satisfies (Isaiah 55:1-2). In the sharing of the
body and blood of Christ, hearts may be converted, persons reconciled, and tears of lamentation turned to joy.
"Your Spirit," the priest says to God in the Eucharistic
prayer for reconciliation, "changes our hearts: enemies
begin to speak to one another, those who were estranged
join hands in friendship, and nations seek the way of
peace."

The practice of the Eucharist is a sacrament of the
communion of all persons in the one body of Christ, a visible sign of an invisible grace. We behold the bread that
earth has given and human hands have made, and we see

the ruby red fruit of the vine. We witness the elevation of the Host and the breaking of the one bread that is Christ's body, and we share the one cup of Christ's blood. What may not be visible in churches that so often mirror the divisions of our fractured society is the ingathering and reconciliation of all peoples at the messianic table. "It is appalling," Rev. Dr. Martin Luther King Jr. lamented, "that the most segregated hour of Christian America is eleven o'clock on Sunday morning."[33]

In the Catholic liturgy, the Eucharistic prayer for reconciliation promises that God will "gather people of every race, language, and way of life to share in the one eternal banquet with Jesus Christ the Lord." This ingathering took visible form at "All Are Welcome? Race in the Church Today," a forum sponsored by the Archdiocese of Cincinnati and the University of Dayton in January 2011. Three hundred people gathered for the event, including members of twenty-five different parishes and nineteen Catholic high schools. Glancing across the polished oak floor of the ballroom at the University of Dayton's Kennedy Center, I saw people of African, Asian, Hispanic, and European descent seated around circular tables.

The forum began with testimony of personal experiences of acts of exclusion and prayers of lament led by Deacon Royce Winters, Director of African American Ministry for the archdiocese. "Like a dry land without water, my soul thirsts for you, my God" (Psalm 63). We heard the story of Raphael Simmons: "I spent time as a teen living in Dayton with my mother and attended an all-white Catholic Church. Well, the white folks wouldn't get near us . . . in church! We stayed in the back, not because we had to, we just didn't feel welcome. They treated us as though we were less of a person than they."

Gerald Beyer of Saint Joseph's University, one of the keynote speakers, cited studies documenting ongoing inequalities in the access of African Americans to education, housing, health care, and employment. Bryan Massingale, author of *Racial Justice in the Catholic Church*, spoke of our socialization into patterns of exclusion and the visceral emotions stirred by the reality of racism, including anger, fear, shame, and weariness. "We are here," he said, "in the tragic brokenness that affects our society and our church. Racism affects us all, and no one is immune from its damage."

At noon in the atrium outside the ballroom, we picked up our lunches, selecting from bright blue bags marked "turkey," "Italian," or "veggie." Each bag included a sandwich, chips, and a large apple. The food was common fare, but it was shared in very uncommon circumstances. As people milled in the hallway, a man of Vietnamese ancestry and an African American man embraced each other. "Hello, brother!" one exclaimed.

Back in the ballroom, I sat beneath gold chandeliers at a round table with five other women—one white and four black. All across the ballroom with its windows draped in red velvet, I could hear the hum and buzz of animated conversation punctuated by laughter. At my own table, we made introductions and discovered that all of us had come from Cincinnati.

I bit into the layers of tortilla, lettuce, and cheese in my sandwich, and Regina and Sandra discussed their ongoing work with the Ladies Auxiliary of the Knights of Peter Claver. They are collecting food for after-school programs, providing meals for guests at Ronald McDonald House, ministering to women in prison, and supporting them in transition to civilian life. Upon invitation, the four African American women at the table described some of their experiences of exclusion, including the feeling of being unwelcome in department stores, and the constant stress of living in a culture of systemic racism, a stress they cannot speak about with white colleagues at work. These mothers and grandmothers expressed their deep appreciation for the education they had received in Catholic schools—and their concern about lack of educational and employment opportunities for their children.

As I bit into the juicy pulp of my gleaming red apple, a tall black woman approached the other white woman at our table and took her hand. "She's my choir director," Anne, the white woman, explained with a smile.

"You're eating a veggie wrap?" Regina said to Joyce across the table, "Are you vegetarian?"

"Yup," she replied.

"What do you eat at home?"

"All kinds of things. Tofu."

"Tofu ain't got no taste."

"You have to marinate it. Give it flavor."

"Do you grow your own veggies?"

"We have a box garden. Don't want to feed the squirrels and rabbits. And I shop in the produce section at the store. When you make a salad, put all the colors in it—something orange, some yellow, some red. Get the Romaine lettuce— not that iceberg—there's nothing to it but water. And stay away from white bread. Do you know what happens when you mix white bread and water? It turns to glue. That's what it does in your stomach."

"You should give us classes on healthy eating!" Regina responded, and then she passed around a bar of chocolate and everyone took a piece.

Lunch was followed by a keynote address by C. Vanessa White, who, following the example of Sr. Thea Bowman, walked down from the podium to bodily move people from one table to another to enhance each circle's diversity.

The event culminated in a Eucharist celebrated by the archbishop. The procession was led by a man bearing a cross upon which hung an African Christ; the reading from Corinthians was done in Spanish; and the recessional hymn was sung in both Zulu and English: "*Siyahamb' ekukhanyen' kwenkhos'*—We are marching in the light of God." We each live in different ways within relationships that have been scarred by the painful histories of human exclusion and injustice. We all shared, nonetheless, in the communion of the one body and blood of Christ. The Eucharist, said Archbishop Schnurr, "is the source and summit of who we are."

I went home thinking about the questions an African American woman had posed in the discussion that followed one of the workshop sessions: "How many of you have ever invited into your home a Catholic who does not look like you? How many of you have ever welcomed them to your table? How many of you have befriended them? That's hope, that's Christianity, that's Catholicism."

Giving Thanks

In America today, I am barraged with voices that urge me to feed my cravings, to take and eat without delay, to consume without ceasing, to act with the assurance that I am entitled to have everything I desire. I am all too ready to oblige. In the biological scheme of things, I am indeed a consumer, helplessly dependent for my own survival on species of life that can produce energy directly from the sun. Encoded in my genes are biological memories of long spells of scarcity and famine, and I instinctively grasp for food with a particular keenness for fat and sugar, storing up my own reserves. I am a daughter of Adam and Eve, and my character and community are shaped by the legacy of their consumption of the forbidden fruit, an act variously interpreted in the Christian tradition as a transgression rooted in pride, disobedience, avarice, gluttony, or fear. My daily consciousness hovers around my own sense of self and my family—the wants, needs, desires, and insecurities of our existence that Martin Heidegger termed a being-unto-death.

As I enter the door of Xavier's Bellarmine Chapel on a Friday afternoon, I am immediately struck by the profundity of the silence. This is a silence that has never been broken by the blare of a television or radio voice assuring me that I truly deserve to purchase and consume everything that is dangled before me. I hear only the stream of water flowing softly from the baptismal font into the pool. Behind the altar hangs an empty cross, and in the side chapel, the Eucharist is reserved in the tabernacle. The gold doors of the tabernacle are open, and on either side stands a candle that bathes everything in a soft glow. On the beige brick of a side wall is a reproduction of André Rublev's icon of the Trinity, inspired by the story of the hospitality offered by Sarah and Abraham to three strangers.

The Eucharist, wrote Thomas Aquinas, is the sacrament "of supreme charity, and the uplifter of our hope."[34] The body and blood of Christ given for us in love is the food of the redemption of the daughters and sons of Adam and Eve. Hadewijch, the thirteenth-century Flemish Beguine and poet, wrote of a desire that cannot be expressed by any language and the aching pain of great separation. In the food offered to her from the ciborium and the chalice, she tasted the communion of her humanity with Christ in whom humanity and divinity are one: "Then it was to me as if we were one without difference. It was thus: outwardly, to see, taste, and feel, as one can outwardly taste, see, and feel in the reception of the outward Sacrament. So can the Beloved, with the loved one, each wholly receive the other in all full satisfaction of the sight, the hearing, and the passing away of one in the other."[35] In "Love's Seven Names," she wrote:

> Love's most intimate union
> Is through eating, tasting and seeing interiorly.
> He eats us; we think we eat him,
> And we do eat him, of this we can be certain.[36]

Eating, comments Caroline Walker Bynum, is the central metaphor of this stanza of the poem, "not merely because the Eucharist is the place in Christian ritual in which God is most intimately received but also because *to eat* and *to be eaten* express that interpenetration and mutual engulfing, that fusion of fleshly humanness with fleshly humanness, that Hadewijch saw as necessary for uniting with a God-who-is-[hu]man."[37]

The form of the Greek word *eucharistein* (Luke 22:19; cf. 1 Corinthians 11:24) used in Luke's account of the Last Supper is translated "he gave thanks." The sacrament of the Eucharist is a thanksgiving for love's most intimate union, a thanksgiving for the food and drink of eternal life that we receive (John 6:54). To give thanks is to receive without grasping, to eat without consuming, to taste without transgressing, and to live in the awareness that both the bread on our tables and the food and drink on the altar are unmerited gifts of the God who is love.

notes

Introduction

1. Robert Putnam, *Bowling Alone: The Collapse and Revival of American Community* (New York: Simon & Schuster, 2000), 100–101.

Chapter 1. Eating and Drinking in America

1. In Nina Luttinger and Gregory Dicum, *The Coffee Book: Anatomy of an Industry from Crop to the Last Drop,* rev. ed. (New York: New, 2006), 7.

2. Ibid., 9.

3. Ibid., ix.

4. Ibid., 55.

5. http://www.consumerreports.org/health/healthy-living/diet-nutrition/healthy-foods/breakfast-cereals/overview/breakfast-cereals-ov.htm (accessed March 20, 2011).

6. Douglas Foster "Covering Coffee Country," interview with Sam Quinones, *FRONTLINE/World,* http://www.pbs.org/frontlineworld/stories/guatemala.mexico/quinones.html (accessed March 3, 2011).

7. Dan Koeppel, *Banana: The Fate of the Fruit That Changed the World* (New York: Hudson Street, 2008), 64.

8. Henning Steinfield and others, *Livestock's Long Shadow: Environmental Issues and Options* (Rome: Food and Agriculture Association of the UN, 2006), xxi; Michael Pollan, *The Omnivore's Dilemma: The Natural History of Four Meals* (New York: Penguin, 2006), 65–68.

9. The Food Empowerment Project, "Slavery in the Chocolate Factory," http://www.foodispower.org/slavery_chocolate.htm (accessed March 3, 2011).

10. Peter Singer and Jim Mason, *The Ethics of What We Eat: Why Our Food Choices Matter* (Emmaus, Pa.: Rodale, 2006), 26.

11. Mary Oliver, "Blue Heron," in *White Pine: Poems and Prose Poems* (Orlando, Fla.: Harcourt Brace, 1994), 20.

Chapter 2. Eating in and Out of Eden

1. Wendell Berry, *The Unsettling of America: Culture and Agriculture* (San Francisco, Calif.: Sierra Club, 1997).

2. David R. Montgomery, *Dirt: The Erosion of Civilizations* (Berkeley: University of California Press, 2007); Dale Allen Pfeiffer, *Eating Fossil Fuels: Oil, Food, and the Coming Crisis in Agriculture* (Gabriola Island, B.C.: New Society, 2006); Paul Roberts, *The End of Food* (Boston: Houghton Mifflin, 2008).

3. Michael Pollan, *In Defense of Food: An Eater's Manifesto* (New York: Penguin, 2008), 10–11, 85–89, 136.

4. Michael Pollan, *The Omnivore's Dilemma* (New York: Penguin, 2006), 5.

5. Barbara Kingsolver, *Animal, Vegetable, Miracle: A Year of Food Life* (New York: Harper Perennial, 2007), 16–17.

6. Ibid., 38.

7. R. Marie Griffith, "The Promised Land of Weight Loss," *Christian Century* 114 (7 May 1997): 448–54.

8. Statisics from the National Eating Disorders Association (NEDA). See www.NationalEatingDisorders.org (accessed March 3, 2011).

9. Ephrem the Syrian, "On Reading the Paradise Narrative," in *Select Poems*, trans. Sebastian P. Brock and George A. Kiraz (Provo, Utah: Brigham Young University Press, 2006), 7.

10. Ibid., 13.

11. In Franklin Kelly, *Thomas Cole's Paintings of Eden* (Fort Worth, Tex.: Amon Carter Museum, 1994), 21.

12. Gregory of Nyssa, "On the Making of Man," trans. William Moore and Henry Austin Wilson, in *Nicene and Post-Nicene Fathers of the Christian Church*, second series, vol. 5 (Grand Rapids, Mich.: Eerdmans, 1988), 1.4.1.

13. Ibid., 1.2.2.

14. Ephrem the Syrian, "On Reading the Paradise Narrative," 11.

15. John of Damascus, "On the Orthodox Faith," trans. S. D. F. Salmond, in *Nicene and Post-Nicene Fathers of the Christian Church*, second series, vol. 9 (Grand Rapids, Mich.: Eerdmans, 1988), 2.11.

16. Ibid., 2.11.

17. Irenaeus, *Proof of the Apostolic Preaching*, trans. Joseph P. Smith, Ancient Christian Writers no. 16 (Westminster, Md.: Newman, 1952), 15.

18. See Matthias Beier, *A Violent God Image: An Introduction to the Work of Eugen Drewermann* (New York: Continuum, 2004).

19. Augustine, *Confessions*, trans. Henry Chadwick (New York: Oxford, 1991), 2.5.10.

20. Elizabeth Theokritoff, *Living in God's Creation: Orthodox Perspectives on Ecology* (Crestwood, N.Y.: St Vladimir's Seminary Press, 2009), 84.

21. Abraham Joshua Heschel, *God in Search of Man: A Philosophy of Judaism* (New York: Noonday, 1955).

22. See Sandy Eisenberg Sasso, *Noah's Wife: The Story of Naamah* (Woodstock, Vt.: Jewish Lights, 1996).

23. *Talmud Sanhedrin* 108b.

24. *Tanchuma*, Noah 4, p. 35.

25. Jacob Milgrom, *Leviticus 1–16: A New Translation with Introduction and Commentary*, Anchor Bible, vol. 3 (New York: Doubleday, 1991), 48.

26. Ellen Davis, *Scripture, Culture, and Agriculture: An Agrarian Reading of the Bible* (New York: Cambridge University Press, 2009), 70.

27. Abraham Joshua Heschel, *Between God and Man* (New York: Free, 1959), 116–24.

28. Heschel, *God in Search of Man*, 325.

29. Ibid., 291.

30. Ibid., 288–89.

31. Ibid., 263–76.

32. Milgrom, *Leviticus: A Book of Ritual and Ethics* (Minneapolis: Fortress Press, 2004), 307.

33. Davis, *Scripture, Culture, and Agriculture*, 94.

34. Milgrom, *Leviticus*, 108.

35. Ibid., 103.

36. Ibid., 8–14.

37. Ibid., 290.

38. Ibid., 1.

39. Ibid., 17.

40. Jacob Neusner, *A Short History of Judaism: Three Meals, Three Epochs* (Minneapolis: Fortress Press, 1992), 19.

41. Heschel, *Between God and Man*, 125.

42. John Dominic Crossan, *The Greatest Prayer* (New York: HarperOne, 2010), 120–25.

43. Monika Hellwig, *Jesus, the Compassion of God* (Wilmington, Del.: Michael Glazier, 1983).

44. Greory of Nazianzus, "The Third Theological Oration: On the Son," trans. Charles Gordon Browne and James Edward Swallow, in *Nicene and Post-Nicene Fathers of the Christian Church*, second series, vol. 7 (Grand Rapids, Mich.: Eerdmans, 1989), 20.

45. John P. Meier, *A Marginal Jew: Rethinking the Historical Jesus*, vol. 2 (New York: Doubleday, 1994), 966.

Chapter 3. The Christian Practice of Eating and Drinking

1. Wendell Berry, "A Defense of the Family Farm," in *Bringing It to the Table: On Farming and Food* (Berkeley: Counterpoint, 2009), 37; Berry, "Christianity and the Survival of Creation," in *The Art of the Commonplace: The Agrarian Essays of Wendell Berry*, ed. Norman Wirzba (Washington, D.C.: Counterpoint, 2002), 308–9.

2. Aristides, *Apology*, 19.9. Cited in Thomas Ryan, *The Sacred of Fasting: Preparing to Practice* (Woodstock, Vt.: Skylight Paths, 2005), 51–52.

3. Thomas Ryan, *Fasting Rediscovered: A Guide to Health and Wholeness for Your Body Spirit* (New York: Paulist, 1981), 20.

4. Charles Murphy, *The Spirituality of Fasting: Rediscovering a Christian Practice* (Notre Dame, Ind.: Ave Maria, 2010), 7.

5. Eamon Duffy, "To Fast Again," *First Things* 151 (March 2005): 4.

6. George Robinson, *Essential Judaism: A Complete Guide to Beliefs, Customs, and Rituals* (New York: Pocket, 2000), 19–22.

7. L. Shannon Jung, *Food for Life* (Minneapolis: Fortress Press, 2004), 97.

8. Food Research and Action Center (FRAC) press release, "New Anaylsis of Food Hardship Shows At Least One in Seven Respondents in Nearly Every State Unable to Afford Enough Food in First Half of 2010" (December 29, 2010). Report available at http://frac.org/reports-and-resources/food-hardship-data/.

9. UN News Service, "Current Global Crises Deepening Hunger Worldwide, Warns UN Agency" (28 May 2009). http://www.un.org/apps/news/story.asp?NewsID=30950&Cr=hunger&Cr1=.

10. United States Conference of Catholic Bishops, "Global Climate Change and Our Catholic Response," http://www.nccbuscc.org/sdwp/globalpoverty/ccgp_issues_climatechange.shtml.

11. UN News Service, "Current Global Crises Deepening."

12. This is the figure given by the Secretary General of the UN. See http://articles.cnn.com/2009-11-17/world/italy.food.summit_1_

food-security-hunger-world-food-program?_s=PM:WORLD (accessed March 3, 2011).

13. Sharman Apt Russell, *Hunger: An Unnatural History* (New York: Basic, 2005), 12.

14. Ibid., 13.

15. John Chrysostom, "Homilies on the Arts of the Apostles," trans. J. Walker, J. Shepperd, and H. Browne, in *Nicene and Post-Nicene Fathers of the Christian Church*, first series, vol. 11 (Grand Rapids, Mich.: Eerdmans, 1974), 45.

16. Paul Roberts, *The End of Food* (Boston: Houghton Mifflin, 2008), 209.

17. Julian Cribb, *The Coming Famine: The Global Food Crisis and What We Can Do to Avoid It* (Berkeley, Calif.: University of California Press, 2010), 33–34, 67, 134.

18. Food and Agriculture Association of the United Nations, *Livestock's Long Shadow* (Rome, 2006).

19. "UN Says to Eat Less Meat to Curb Global Warming," *Guardian,* September 7, 2008, http://www.guardian.co.uk/environment /2008/sep/07/food.foodanddrink (accessed March 3, 2011).

20. *Mystical Treatises by Isaac the Syrian*, translated from the Syriac text by Bedjan Koninklijke (Amsterdam: Akademie van Westenschappen te Amsterdam, 1923), cited in Vladimir Lossky, *The Mystical Theology of the Eastern Church* (Cambridge and London: James Clarke, 1944, 1957), 111.

21. Cardinal Joseph Ratzinger, *God and the World: A Conversation with Peter Seewald* (San Francisco: Ignatius, 2002), 78–79.

22. Michael Pollan, *The Omnivore's Dilemma: A Natural History of Four Meals* (New York: Penguin, 2006), 305.

23. Mark Bitten, *Food Matters: A Guide to Conscious Eating* (New York: Simon & Schuster, 2009), 16.

24. Samson Dressner, *The Jewish Dietary Laws: Their Meaning for Our Time* (New York: Burning Bush, 1966), 24.

25. Samuel Raphael Hirsch, *Horeb: A Philosophy of Jewish Laws and Observances*, trans. I. Grunfeld (London: Soncino, 1962), 317–18.

26. Abraham Isaac Kook, *The Lights of Penitence, The Moral Principles, Lights of Holiness, Essays, Letters, and Poems*, trans. Ben Zion Bokser (New York: Paulist, 1978), 317–23.

27. John P. Meier, *A Marginal Jew: Rethinking the Historical Jesus*, vol. 4, *Law and Love* (New Haven: Yale University Press, 2009), 394.

28. Ephrem the Syrian, *Hymns on Paradise*, trans. Sebastian Brock (Crestwood, N.Y.: St. Vladimir's Seminary Press, 1998), 9.1.

29. Julian Cribb, *The Coming Famine,* xi.

30. Chensheng Lu et al., "Organic Diets Significantly Lower Children's Dietary Exposure to Organophosphorus Pesticides," *Environmental Health Perspectives* 114 (February 2006), 260–63; Kevin Clarke, "Not-So-Special Delivery: Sometimes the Toxic Waste is Not Just in Babies' Diapers," *U.S. Catholic* 70 (October 2005), 41; John Wargo, *Our Children's Toxic Legacy: How Science and the Law Fail to Protect Us from Pesticides* (New Haven: Yale University Press, 1996).

31. Dale Allen Pfeiffer, *Eating Fossil Fuels* (Gabriola Island, Canada: New Society, 2006).

32. Cribb, *The Coming Famine,* 106.

33. Martin Luther King Jr., *Stride Toward Freedom: The Montgomery Story,* 1958 (San Francisco: HarperCollins, 1986), 207.

34. Thomas Aquinas, *Summa Theologiae* III, q. 75, a. 1, ad. c.

35. Hadewijch, "Vision 7: Oneness in the Eucharist," in *Hadewijch: The Complete Works,* trans. Mother Columba Hart (New York: Paulist, 1980), 280–81.

36. "Love's Seven Names," in *Hadewijch: The Complete Works,* 353.

37. Caroline Walker Bynum, *Holy Feast and Holy Fast: The Religious Significance of Food to Medieval Women* (Berkeley: University of California Press, 1987), 156.

suggestions for further reading

The titles listed here are some of the sources used by the author and suggestions for further reading.

Berry, Wendell. *The Unsettling of America: Culture and Agriculture.* San Francisco: Sierra Club, 1997.

Bittman, Mark. *Food Matters: A Guide to Conscious Eating.* New York: Simon & Schuster, 2009.

Cribb, Julian. *The Coming Famine: The Global Food Crisis and What We Can Do to Avoid It.* Berkeley: University of California Press, 2010.

Davis, Ellen. *Scripture, Culture, and Agriculture: An Agrarian Reading of the Bible.* New York: Cambridge University Press, 2009.

Grassi, Joseph. *Broken Bread and Broken Bodies: The Lord's Supper and World Hunger.* Maryknoll, N.Y.: Orbis, 2004.

Hellwig, Monika. *The Eucharist and the Hunger of the World,* 2nd ed. Kansas City: Sheed & Ward, 1992.

Jones, Deborah. *The School of Compassion: A Roman Catholic Theology of Animals.* Herefordshire: Gracewing, 2009.

Jung, L. Shannon. *Food for Life: The Spirituality and Ethics of Eating.* Minneapolis: Fortress Press, 2004.

Kass, Leon. *The Hungry Soul: Eating and the Perfection of Our Nature.* Chicago: University of Chicago Press, 1994, 1999.

Lappé, Anna. *Diet for a Hot Planet: The Climate Crisis at the End of Your Fork and What You Can Do about It*. New York: Bloomsbury, 2010.

Mendez Montoya, Angel F. *Theology of Food: Eating and the Eucharist*. Malden, Mass.: Wiley-Blackwell, 2009.

Murphy, Charles M. *The Spirituality of Fasting: Rediscovering a Christian Practice*. Notre Dame, Ind.: Ave Maria, 2010.

Pollan, Michael. *The Omnivore's Dilemma: A Natural History of Four Meals*. New York: Penguin, 2006.

———. "Farmer in Chief." *New York Times Magazine*, October 12, 2008, 62–71 and ff.

Roberts, Paul. *The End of Food*. Boston: Houghton Mifflin, 2008.

Rubio, Julie Hanlon. *Family Ethics: Practices for Christians*. Washington, D.C.: Georgetown University Press, 2010.

Ryan, Thomas. *Fasting Rediscovered: A Guide to Health and Wholeness for Your Body-Spirit*. New York: Paulist, 1981.

Walker Bynum, Caroline. *Holy Feast and Holy Fast: The Religious Significance of Food to Medieval Women*. Berkeley: University of California Press, 1987.

reader's guide

1. Select one of the foods you eat regularly and learn what you can about its provenance. Where was it grown? Who grew it? How was it cultivated? How did it get from its place of origin to your kitchen? What theological or ethical questions or insights arise from your investigation?

2. Visit a local farmers' market—or, if none exists, try to start one in your church parking lot. Interview the farmers about their experience. What are the joys and challenges of their vocation? What theological or spiritual insights might they offer as they reflect on their experience of working closely with the land?

3. Which biblical accounts of eating and drinking are most striking to you? What do you think is their meaning and significance? How do biblical practices of eating and drinking compare with our own?

4. What is your assessment of Michael Pollan's position that the United States is a country with a "national eating disorder"? Do you see any evidence of this? Or evidence to the contrary?

5. Cribb, Roberts, Pollan, Berry, and others warn that we have reached a point of severe crisis in our food system. What is your diagnosis of the underlying causes of this crisis? How can Christian churches contribute to a constructive response?

6. Have you ever experienced an extended period of hunger for food? What was it like? What other forms of

hunger do you experience? What are your deepest desires? How do our various desires and hungers overlap?

7. What are the theological and ethical reasons for abstinence from eating meat or animal products? What are the theological and ethical reasons that support eating meat or animal products? What is your own practice in this regard, and why?

8. What principles and vision should guide our nation's food and agricultural policies? With a group from your parish, engage elected representatives at the local, regional, and national levels in conversation on this topic.

9. Is your church's celebration of the Eucharist or Lord's Supper a visible sign of the messianic communion of people of all nations? If so, how do you experience this? If not, how can your practice of table fellowship become a closer approximation of the messianic feast?

10. Do you have a contemplative practice such as Eucharistic adoration or centering prayer? How might a practice such as this shape our daily practices of eating and drinking?